# Chaitanya Mahaprabhu

# Chaitanya Mahaprabhu

## The Story of Bengal's Greatest Bhakti Saint

Chitrita Banerji

JUGGERNAUT BOOKS
C-I-128, First Floor, Sangam Vihar, Near Holi Chowk,
New Delhi 110080, India

First published in hardback by Juggernaut Books 2018
Published in paperback 2022



10 9 8 7 6 5 4 3

P-ISBN: 9789391165970
E-ISBN: 9789393986122



Typeset in Adobe Caslon Pro by R. Ajith Kumar, Noida

Printed at Thomson Press India Ltd

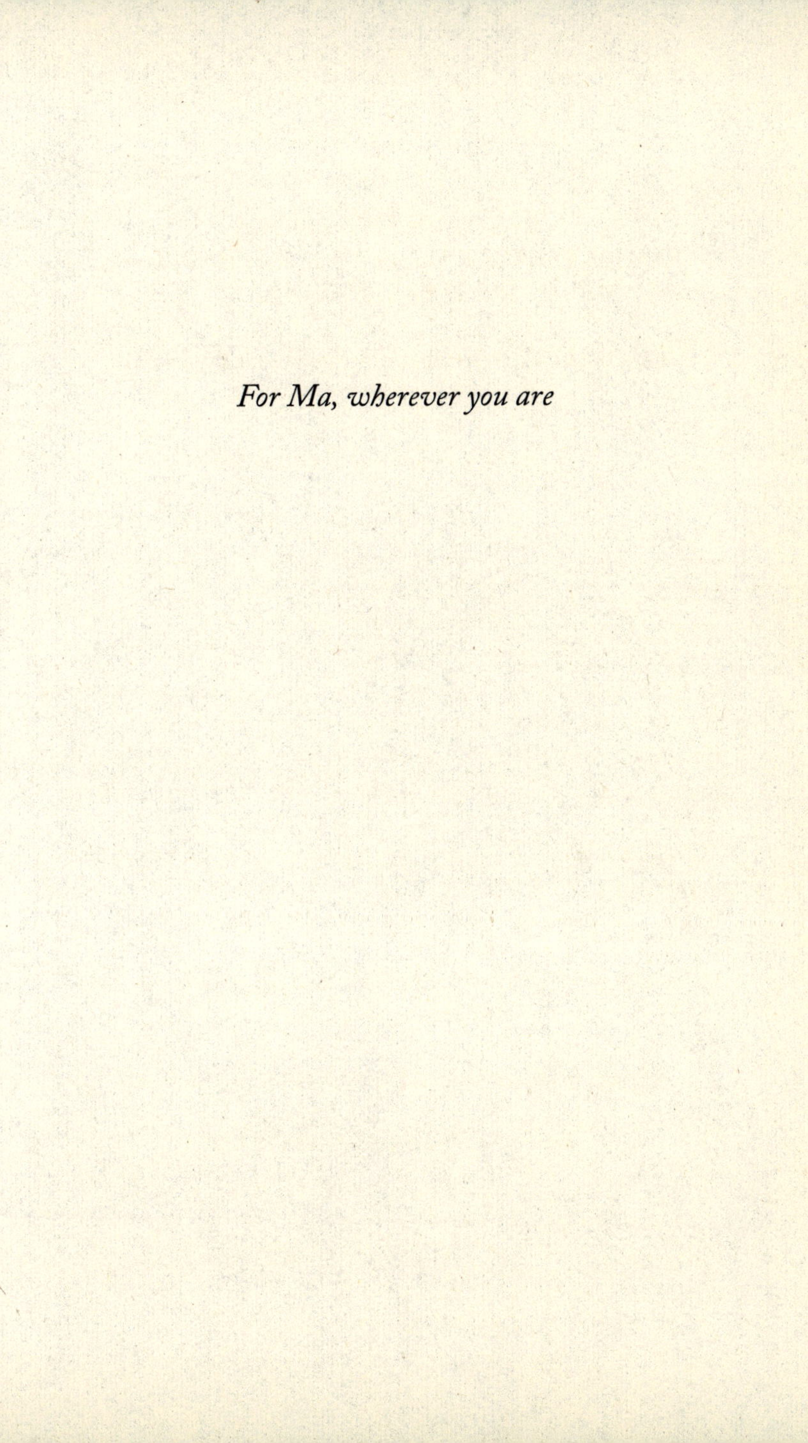

*For Ma, wherever you are*

# Contents

# Author's Note

This is not a scholarly biography of Chaitanya. Rather, it is an attempt to present his life as a story which appeals to people more than five centuries after his birth. The earliest accounts of Chaitanya's life and times, written either by contemporaries or younger people who knew him well, are more hagiographies than biographies. However, they contain valuable information and details about the man and his message, the important events of his life and the significant steps he took on his journey towards becoming a transformative religious figure. The two best-known works are the *Chaitanya Bhagavat* by Brindaban Das and the *Chaitanya Charitamrita* by Krishnadas Kabiraj. Both provide intimate, human details about Chaitanya, including his youthful high spirits, the warmth of his relationships with friends and followers, the depth of his affection for his mother, the food that he appreciated and enjoyed eating with his disciples, and his deeply immersive love for Krishna – all of which add immediacy and realism to a figure who lived in medieval Bengal but still remains an iconic presence in Bengali culture, faith and history, regardless of whether he is perceived as a god or a man.

# Prologue

In our house the flowers of the kadam tree were the most abiding, pleasurable symbols of the monsoon. Spherical, saffron-coloured clusters of tiny blooms, they filled the damp air with a scent that was sweet without being cloying, and lasted throughout the season. The tree itself was a remarkable specimen, three stories tall, with a rugged trunk encircled by a stone altar my grandfather had built. When it was in full bloom, the dark-green foliage, profusely dotted with round blossoms, under the deep slate-grey of the monsoon sky was a sight that many passers-by stopped to admire.

It was the presence of the tree that had made my grandfather purchase the extensive parcel of land on which he built his house. In Vaishnav literature, the kadam is an integral part of the legends about Krishna. Countless descriptions of

Krishna as a child playing under the kadam, of him as a young man flirtatiously engaging with gopis or milkmaids, waiting for his beloved Radha as he sat under the kadam and played seductive melodies on his flute, or swaying with her on a flower-decked swing attached to a kadam branch on the night of the full moon have accrued to lend a spiritual–mythical aura to a beautiful tree. For a devout Vaishnav like my grandfather, this particular kadam was an auspicious emblem, perhaps an indicator of divine blessing for the family.

By the time I was born, the tree had become the central pillar in a walled garden that was bordered by smaller trees and shrubs, with an area in the middle that was meticulously kept free of vegetation. Several times a year, this space would see an assembly of people – my grandfather's friends, colleagues and associates – who gathered for singing kirtan or Vaishnav devotional music. During the rainy season, a makeshift canopy was erected to protect the singers, the musical instruments and the rough carpets on which they sat. Some of the music consisted of pala kirtan, derived from medieval Bengali lyrics about

Krishna and his beloved Radha in Brindaban, or Brajadham, as it was often called. But most of the time the singers lifted their voices to perform naam kirtan, a repetitive chant of Hare Krishna, Hare Rama, set to beautiful ragas appropriate to the hour of the day or night. On special festive occasions, as on that of Jhulan, which took place in the middle of the monsoon season, these sessions would last for twenty-four hours – from late morning to the morning of the following day. The singers and instrument players took turns, coming inside the house for rest and refreshment. Participation was entirely democratic, including both trained singers and rank amateurs, even those who could barely hold a tune. Out of consideration for our non-Vaishnav neighbours, no instrumental accompaniments were used after midnight and even the singers lowered their voices as much as possible.

As a child, I eagerly awaited these twenty-four-hour music fests which kept the adults, especially my mother, grandmother and aunts, totally preoccupied. They were responsible (with the help of the servants) for creating lavish vegetarian meals that were offered to all who came.

The enveloping redolence of the food – especially that of the cinnamon–cardamom–ginger–ghee-scented khichuri – blending with the sound of music from the garden created, for me, a realm transformed. Our house, normally filled with the vociferous racket of a contentious, often angry family, became a strangely serene space.

Before each twenty-four-hour kirtan session, my grandmother would go down to the garden to set up the altar under the kadam with the appropriate religious symbols, and I always went with her to watch. A simple alpana pattern was painted on the altar with rice flour paste. Incense sticks were lit and wreathed the kadam trunk in fragrant wisps of smoke. Two glass-fronted paintings, brought from the house, were propped up against the tree trunk to face the space where the singers would sit. My grandmother draped each with a thick garland of tuberoses and I was allowed to arrange kadam flowers and their glossy leaves in front of them. One painting was of Krishna and Radha, he draped in a yellow dhoti and she in a night-blue sari, entwined by the symbol of Om. The other depicted a man wearing a saffron dhoti, a scarf round his neck, his face raised to the sky, arms lifted above his shaven head which indicated his monkhood. His eyes half-closed and his lips curved in a gentle smile gave his face an expression of rapture that seemed to belong to another world. To me, he was an intriguing and fascinating figure, for although a man, he was worshipped along with Krishna the god. How could that be, I often wondered. Each time I asked, my grandmother would tell me stories about a man who was born centuries ago in an ordinary Brahmin family like ours and who experienced extraordinary revelations that led him to an awareness of Krishna that was so potent and so intimate that it almost made him the same as Krishna. His name was Chaitanya, or, as she called him, Chaitanya Deb – Chaitanya the god.

No matter how often I heard these stories, I still wondered how a man could become a god. Inside the house, a different portrait, hanging in my grandparents' bedroom, further complicated the issue. In this one, Chaitanya, looking heavenward, stood beside a man dressed in a similar saffron dhoti, with his eyes focused on Chaitanya. The expression on this second man's face was nothing short of adoration, and yet it was different from the intense, otherworldly exaltation that marked Chaitanya's face. He was Nityananda, the best-known disciple/follower/friend of Chaitanya, according to my grandmother. And I found it intriguing that she did not consider him a god, even though his connection with Chaitanya was intimate enough for them to be called brothers. At the beginning of each kirtan session, in the garden or in the house, the lead performers always sang an invocation, not to Krishna himself, but to these two men, affectionately given the names of Gour and Nitai, asking them to bless the assembly and accept the adoration of the singers and devotees. The invocation was purely vocal. None of the instruments – harmonium, khol and/or pakhawaj (drums), chiming cymbals or the stringed esraj – was used as accompaniment. It always had a magical effect of silencing all surrounding clamour, as listeners and performers readied themselves for the kirtan to come. And when that started, the chorus of voices and instruments rising to the sky through the branches of the kadam inevitably sent a thrill through me.

I was not allowed to go into the garden once the singing commenced. But on lesser occasions, when a smaller group of singers gathered in the large room on the first floor for an evening of kirtan, I had the freedom to stand near the door or sit quietly in a corner of the room and listen until it was my bedtime. The music was no less thrilling inside the house. And there was the added fascination of being able to observe the people who were there. As they sang through the evening hours, the Hare Krishna chant rose and fell in countless melodic variations, while the khol players sometimes stood up to perform extraordinarily intricate beats, each responding to the others as if a dialogue was being carried on in parallel to the singing. And sooner or later – this is what I anticipated most eagerly – several singers would also stand, raise their arms just like Chaitanya in the painting and start swaying hypnotically to the rhythm of the music. Most were men, and no one in the family found it odd or comic to watch these normally serious, middle-aged or elderly professionals, some of them still wearing the jacket and tie they had worn to work, abandon themselves to such an intensity of spiritual expression. But there was also a woman, her affluence evident from her glittering jewellery and expensive saris, who had no qualms about casting aside traditional decorum and joining the dancers. Her way of wearing the sari provoked subdued smiles among the women in my family. The shoulder end was always much too long and almost swept the ground like a train as she walked – something of which she seemed supremely unaware. As she swayed to the music, her intense absorption, her half-closed eyes and the slight smile that curved her lips gave her a look that was almost exotic, markedly different from the primness and reserve that marked the faces of the other women present. One of my uncles referred to her as the golden doe, after the magical creature described in the Ramayana. But another gave her a moniker we all adopted – The Duchess. Despite finding her slightly ridiculous, I could not deny her fascinating quality. It was always a disappointment when she didn't show up.

The evenings ended with the joyful, celebratory practice called 'harir loot'. My grandmother would come in with a large brass platter containing batashas – small candies made with dropped sugar syrup – and throw up handfuls into the air. As the batashas came down like confetti, all the participants went down on their hands and knees, trying to gather as many as possible. An element of friendly competition was on display even as grown men and women were overcome with childlike merriment. I had an edge in this game of capture, being the smallest and nimblest person on the ground. When my grandmother's platter was empty, I always had more batashas than anybody else – my loot, my booty, my gift from the lord – nestling in my skirt which I had gathered up like a pouch.

The central figure in most of these performances, however, was a man who never got up, never raised his arms, nor displayed any overt religious emotions. He sat on a small carpet, usually bare-chested except for the sacred thread, his lean body held ramrod-straight, the expression on his hollow-cheeked face one of deep concentration. This was my grandfather's guru, a man of ascetic habits and intense spirituality. I don't know when the two had first met, but whenever he came to stay at our house, all the energy seemed to flow out of everyone and be concentrated around him. He never stayed for long. A few days' visit would be followed by an extended absence before the next one. But I noticed that during those few days, there were no arguments or open discord between my uncles and aunts. He had inducted my grandfather in the faith and practice of Vaishnavism as preached by Chaitanya, a faith based on bhakti or loving devotion instead of rigid asceticism or elaborate ritual. As a child, I did not know what exactly this meant, but what entranced me about him was that he was a writer and composer of the most exquisite lyrics about Chaitanya. Aside from the traditional kirtans, my family also frequently sang these songs which conjured up images of a beautiful, self-forgetful seeker. Trying to visualize a man so in love with the divine that his face was continuously bathed with tears of longing as he walked the streets looking for his beloved, I felt a love for Chaitanya that was sustained by the pure ardour of childhood, even though faith and reverence were too complex for me.

~

Many years later, when I had stopped looking at the world with the simple regard of a child, when my grandfather and his guru were long gone, when the enormous house echoed with emptiness instead of song and most of my grandfather's children, including my parents, had moved away, when the garden had become overrun with shrubs and weeds, when large cracks on the altar surrounding the kadam were filled with dirt and insects, and it was hard to imagine a robust assembly of singers sitting in front of the tree – I found myself wondering about Chaitanya and his enduring presence in the lives of so many people. Those who used to come to our house for the kirtan constituted only a small sample of Bengali Vaishnavs who regard Chaitanya with devotion. But the sample consisted of widely disparate characters. Among the ones I remember was a high court judge, several eminent physicians, a construction magnate (whom I called Engineer Dadu), two barristers, several professor colleagues of my grandfather's, as well as people from lower economic and social strata, including government clerks, a small bookstore owner, even a man who acted as a middleman for fish vendors in Gariahat market and supplied fish for every wedding in our extended family (our vegetarianism was confined only to the days of the kirtan performances). How my grandfather had met all these people and persuaded them to participate in singing kirtan in his house I never learned, but I was absolutely sure that outside the boundaries of those musical gatherings their unity dissolved. Class, education and money determined who mingled socially with whom. Still, it was no mean achievement, I reflected, to bring together people from such varied strata of society and have them assemble in a joyful, ecstatic musical act of devotion. And I also understood that, though my grandfather may have been the catalyst, it was the love and devotion for Chaitanya and his message that bonded them across their differences. This was the Vaishnav equivalent of a Christian congregation in church. It was a way of worship that may have been radical in Chaitanya's time, but was fortuitously in sync with ours. Its simplicity, so different from the baroque orthodoxy of ritualistic Hinduism, and its exhortation for the individual to discover a direct path to god have stayed relevant for a significant cross-section of people over the past five centuries.

Of the many things my grandmother repeatedly told me about Chaitanya, one made a particularly strong impression – that he made no distinctions between people on the basis of class, caste, wealth or even religion. In the room where she worshipped Krishna and Radha, she would point to the reprint of a painting by a famous Bengali artist that showed Chaitanya sitting with one of his favourite followers, an elderly Muslim man who had taken the name of Haridas. What could be a greater indication of the independence of mind that characterized Chaitanya, a Brahmin living in medieval times when no one questioned the caste system, when 'untouchable' and 'outcaste' were categories that aroused no outrage, when Hindu Bengal was under the rule of Muslim sultans and there were frequent conflicts between the two communities? Some of his more orthodox disciples may have disapproved of the extent of his liberality, just as some of my family members as well as many of the kirtan participants in our house would have found it unacceptable to flout significant social norms. Still, it is possible that their adoration of Chaitanya occasionally aroused a wish to emulate his generosity and acceptance of his fellow human beings. Or so I like to think.

Leaving childhood and teenage behind and

moving away from my grandparents' house, I found myself rapidly becoming immersed in the world outside where the opinions of contemporaries and teachers exerted far greater influence than those of family members. The social turbulence of the 1960s and 1970s and the rising pre-eminence of leftist ideas created an immense distance between me and the tender, emotive religiosity of my Vaishnav grandparents. Moreover, this was a time when I was first exposed to an opposite perspective – an intense negativity about Vaishnavs that prevailed among many people. Kirtan, instead of simply being religious music, was also associated with courtesans and demi-mondaines. The Hare Krishna chant was something that provoked ridicule. Vaishnav couples who moved around the city singing kirtans to earn a living were derisively referred to as Boshtom–Boshtumi, the contempt tinged with a distinct moral disapproval. Influenced by such trends, I lost sight of the vivid, lovable man-god whose story had been integrated into my early life. Buffeted by the exigencies of adult life and the passing of older family members, I hardly ever thought of Chaitanya or the extraordinary boldness of his message, even when I listened to exquisite recordings of kirtans by professional singers.

Still, the deepest influences of the past survive years of distraction, inattention and rejection, waiting to be resurrected at unexpected moments – as I discovered when I scandalized my family by marrying a Bengali Muslim, someone who would have been categorized by Hindu society as unacceptable and untouchable in Chaitanya's time and even in ours. All my relatives considered it a disgraceful alliance, even if they did not go as far as severing ties with me. Overwhelmed by the reproach and anger directed at me, I wondered how I would reconfigure the familial ties I had always taken for granted. The answer came in a letter my grandmother wrote to me. The letter is now lost, but I can still see the blue aerogramme paper covered with her exquisite copperplate writing. She addressed me as her beloved grandchild and said she had heard about my marriage with great joy. She hoped to meet my husband when we came to visit from the US, and she was sure she would love him since I had chosen to marry him. She looked forward to telling him stories about my childhood and also the stories that she used to tell me, as a way of making him part of our family. In the end, she reminded me of the lessons to be learned from the life and acts of Chaitanya – that love and acceptance of our fellow human beings help us walk on the road to finding the greatest treasure of all, the love of Krishna.

~

It has been many years since then. Although I cannot say I have followed the path she urged me to tread, her words have stayed with me, rising in my mind during quiet moments and urging me to learn a little more about the person who created a new way of worship, forged a personal link with the god he loved and shaped the thinking of so many in Bengal. Given the long history of Vaishnavism in Bengal, it is only natural that the pendulum of public opinion will sway from one extreme to the other, especially as a society is impacted by the beliefs and philosophies of other cultures. Still, it is very likely that the Vaishnavism preached by Chaitanya, the cornerstone of which is the importance of bhakti or pure devotion over other spiritual modes of striving, never lost its appeal in the villages and rural communities of Bengal. For not only was it a message of spiritual salvation, it was also a message of social cohesion and uplift. The poorest of the poor could aspire to be one with Krishna if only they could seek him with true bhakti and chant his name as a way of worship. Such an idea freed them from the tyranny of the priestly class who could declare a person an outcaste even for some minor infringement of religious practice, and who often demanded money and gifts to perform rituals that would either bring salvation or atone for sins they had committed. It was all the more remarkable because Chaitanya himself, unlike, say, another medieval reformer like Kabir, was the son of a Brahmin whose father and ancestors had accepted the value of rituals and some degree of orthodoxy. What mattered was that when the average, struggling Bengali peasants, tradesmen or lower-caste and untouchable workers looked at Chaitanya they did not just see a person of the highest caste, whose relatives and peers had been used to teaching abstruse academic disciplines and performing elaborate priestly functions for centuries. Nor did they see an aggressive social reformer or revolutionary zealot intent on breaking down a society based on the caste system. Instead, what they saw was a man whose message was centred on man's relationship with the divine, who expressed an astonishing degree of liberality and an all-inclusive embrace of humanity with all its frailties and imperfections. As they were lifted up by his words, they also identified with him on a visceral level as the son of a loving mother, a man wearing a simple dhoti and scarf, a man who loved to eat the same kind of food as they did, whose lessons did not baffle them with the dry intellectualism of well-known scholars and pandits, who projected the emotional warmth of a friend. The aristocracy of birth in caste-dominated Hindu society seemed of no account when Chaitanya the Brahmin spoke to a lowly leather worker, sweeper or even a Muslim.

Over the centuries, Chaitanya's appeal may have waned, especially among the more prosperous, urban classes, who found the intense emotionalism of his message somewhat off-putting, particularly because they were increasingly influenced by Western ideas. But his voice and presence were never totally extinguished, and as colonial Bengal edged into the late twentieth and early twenty-first centuries, scholars and historians began to find a new way of assessing him. His boldness in simplifying a religious message, his deep love and appreciation of literature (the lyrical works of poets like Joydeb, Vidyapati and Chandidas), his gift for singing, dancing and performing – all combined to give him a resplendence that was typically Bengali and not of any other place. This image of believable exceptionalism, quite distinct from that of a superhuman visionary or a man made mad by his love for the divine, re-enshrined Chaitanya in the hearts and minds of a new category of Bengalis. The particular love and adoration for Chaitanya that motivated my grandfather, his guru and his cohorts are likely to have grown out of this phenomenon.

~

Whatever the validity of such retrospective assessments, I still feel that the continued presence of Chaitanya as a Bengali icon is deeply rooted in the story of an individual life – a life of humble beginnings that is transformed into a marvellous example of spirituality, human empathy and a seemingly infinite capacity for love, a life that leads to the propagation of a message that can lend itself to intellectual appreciation as well as immediate emotional acceptance. It is a story that entwines marvels, miracles and transformation within the boundaries of quintessential humanity. It is a story that begins on a night of eclipse in a small town by the river . . .

# Part One

# Nimai

# 1

# Advent

When one of her friends asks if she can hear the noise outside, Shachi thinks the woman is referring to the rustling of the branches of the neem tree that stands near her house. In the spring, its branches are laden with small, coppery leaves with serrated edges and the wind that passes through them is supposed to benefit anyone who sits underneath, while the leaves themselves are supposed to have medicinal properties. Exhausted with the intense pain of ongoing labour, Shachi can only nod. She has not heard the other, distant noise that her friend was referring to.

The room is dark, completely sealed off from external light and air and illuminated by a few oil lamps. But after hours of suffering, Shachi has lost sense of the difference between outside and inside. She drifts into a strange dreamworld, where the past seems as real as the present. She has already lived through the tragedy of losing children – eight babies, each of whom died soon after birth. Her eldest child, a son called Biswarup, is now eleven, but instead of behaving like a normal boy, he has become preternaturally reclusive, burying himself in books and showing a precocious interest in matters ascetic and spiritual. She worries about what direction his life will take. And now, as she prepares to welcome another life, she can't help wondering anxiously what fate will bring her.

During the long hours while she awaits this birth, Shachi keeps remembering the arduous trek she has made only a short time ago to the ancestral home of her in-laws. A distance of nearly 300 miles as the crow flies separates the village of Dhaka Dakhhin in the eastern Bengali district of Sylhet from the town of Nabadwip on the bank of the Ganga. Nabadwip is the beloved town that Shachi considers home, where she has spent her childhood, and where she has lived as a wife and mother. The mere prospect of making her way through untamed landscapes and unfamiliar towns, navigating rivers and other large waterbodies in order to reach Dhaka Dakhhin where her parents-in-law still live was unnerving. Yet, halfway through this pregnancy, when her in-laws asked her to come and stay with them and give birth to her child in their ancestral home, she had no way to refuse. Especially after all the disappointment she had caused them by losing so many babies. As a dutiful daughter-in-law, she acquiesced to her mother-in-law's demand. Yet, here she is now, back from Dhaka Dakhhin, because her mother-in-law had a strange dream in which she saw that her grandchild was destined to be born in Nabadwip. Between her personal anxieties and the stress of travelling back and forth, it has been a strange few months. Now, in this small, dark room, Shachi intensely longs for an end to her ordeal and to be the mother of a healthy child.

~

Outside, it is a beautiful spring evening, the evening of 18 February 1486. A balmy breeze raises gentle ripples on the surface of the Ganga as it glints under the silver luminescence of a full moon. To the residents of Nabadwip, there is no life without the Ganga. It provides the water essential for daily needs and, more important, bathing in the river is supposed to wash away one's sins. Morning and evening, the river's ghats are crowded with bathers young and old, male and female. It is a place to meet friends, neighbours and colleagues; a place to relax away from home, watch the merchant ships and small rowboats make their way down the river; to catch up on the day's news, exchange confidences with close friends and savour the freedom of being away from the confines of domesticity. For mischievous children, it provides ample opportunity to engage in pranks – sprinkling water on fresh clothes a bather has left on the ghat while he is in the river, or hiding a scholar's books and papers, or scattering the sacred ingredients a person has assembled to conduct ritual worship. The Ganga and its ghats constitute the heartbeat of Nabadwip.

But on this night a sudden blight strikes the world. A shadow advances and covers the moon, plunging the town into an eerie darkness. It is a full lunar eclipse and no one knows what evil it might portend. Terrified residents start wailing, praying, prostrating themselves on the river ghats, and asking the deities to save them from unknown calamity. Their voices, loudly chanting the names of Krishna and Hari, fill the air.

In the darkness of the birthing room, the darkness of the eclipse makes no difference. It is the sound of prayers and chanting that reaches the women attending Shachi and makes them fearful about what is happening. But not for long. For soon the child they have been waiting for enters the world – a beautiful, golden boy. Shachi holds her blessed baby and prays for his life and health. Her friends, aware of the tragic loss of eight previous babies, suggest that whatever formal name he may be given, he should commonly be called Nimai, after the neem tree outside the house, a tree whose leaves, although beneficial in so many ways, taste so bitter that even death avoids them. A beautiful baby will be protected from the evil eye by the repelling power of this nickname. Shachi agrees, although she and her husband have also thought of a formal name if the child is a boy – Biswambhar, he who fills the world. He will fill her world if he lives.

Neither she nor anyone else knows at this time that in the future he will become a man of many names. Some will fondly call him Gour, Gora, or Gouranga, because of his golden complexion. With the passage of time, he will become inextricably entwined with his home town, as people refer to him as Nader Nimai (since Nabadwip will also be known as Nadia). And in his early twenties, he will take on a new name and identity – Krishna Chaitanya. What is also impossible for anyone to know this night is that his arrival signals the beginning of a marvellous journey of faith, devotion, joy and inclusiveness that will live on for centuries.

Tonight, though, he just lies in his mother's arms, listening to her beating heart, filling her world. She dreams of the future where her baby will flourish and she will nurture both her sons with the dishes she cooks to perfection and a love that is endless, unconditional.

# 2

# Place and Time

Nabadwip – a new island or perhaps a combination of nine islands? Names have varying legends, some of which are lost in the mists of time. When Nimai enters the world, Nabadwip lies on the eastern bank of the Ganga. In a deltaic territory like Bengal, the landscape is fragile, repeatedly fractured by the unpredictable movements of the rivers. Cities and towns take shape as rivers veer in different directions and throw up fragments of land that form islets. Over time, some of the islets merge and create areas large enough for human habitation. Many such formations have appeared and disappeared in the course of the centuries, just as rivers have morphed into narrow channels or widened into huge waterways or simply disappeared, leaving behind sandy beds as the only sign of their one-time presence. The Ganga, it is believed, has been there since ancient times, a witness to the birth, growth and death of towns. Nabadwip is one of her creations.

By the end of the fifteenth century, the town not only has a long history, it has also become an important centre of urban life. It is known throughout the kingdom of Bengal, east and west, as a notable seat of commercial and cultural endeavour. Although the town of Gaur has been the capital of Bengal for several successive ruling dynasties, Nabadwip has a special cachet. A bird's-eye view reveals a flourishing area, with houses bordering the river as well as densely populated neighbourhoods and busy markets stretching farther inland. Four important ghats provide access to the Ganga – Apon Ghat, Madhaier Ghat, Barkona Ghat and Nagariya Ghat. Nimai's parental home, like those of many priests and scholars, is situated near Apon Ghat. Further inland are the homes of merchants and traders whose business is conducted in the different markets. Numerous temples, small and large, are crowded with devotees who come to worship their respective deities, make offerings and watch the priests conduct sacred rituals. Evening echoes with the sound of temple bells.

The prosperity of Nabadwip is built on the local and international trade in items like cotton, fine silk textiles, conch shell products, mangoes and many other goods from Bengal that are heavily in demand elsewhere. The Ganga and its tributaries serve as conduits for this trade, downward to the Bay of Bengal, upward to the northern regions of India. Sitting on the steps of the river ghats, the citizens of Nabadwip watch the majestic progress of ships adorned with peacock-shaped prows, their proud sails fluttering in the breeze as they travel with their valuable cargo. In their long, frothy wakes, smaller boats and barges tremble and sway, but they too make their way to farms and markets and local piers.

Material affluence, however, is a secondary factor in Nabadwip's fame. Throughout the kingdom, and even outside, the town is known as a centre of intellectual excellence because of the large number of Brahmin scholars who have chosen to settle here. Some of them are local, but many have come from distant parts of Bengal, as far east as Chittagong and Sylhet, and even from the neighbouring province of Tripura. Individually or in groups, they have created private academies where they instruct boys and young men in the traditional disciplines of grammar and philosophy as well as the more esoteric doctrines of tantra, nyaya and smriti. From time to time, they get together and engage in scholastic debates, each intent on proving his intellectual superiority. Given the limited income one can make by teaching, most of them also need to augment their resources by conducting priestly rituals for the town residents. Since their lives revolve around the scriptural and the sacerdotal, it is only natural that they should be drawn to live close to the banks of the holy Ganga.

~

For Vaishnav migrants who have come to Nabadwip from Sylhet, travel has not been easy. Not only did they have to traverse a significant distance, they also had to be prepared to encounter sudden, unseasonable floods and storms. But the interconnected river system provides a more dependable route than any by land, given the many undeveloped, forested areas along the way where bandits and thugs prey on travellers. The Jalangi, a tributary of the Ganga, flows from Nabadwip into the mighty Padma in eastern Bengal, which in turn branches into smaller rivers that join the enormous lakes and wetlands so typical of the topography of Sylhet. Shachi had to travel back and forth along these same watery conduits when she visited her in-laws before Nimai's birth. Her son, too, will make the same journey one day.

The proximity to the Ganga is not, however, the chief reason for which the members of Nimai's paternal and maternal family have chosen to leave behind their ancestral homes in Sylhet. The difficult decision to upend themselves and move hundreds of miles westward is the result of a spate of natural disasters, including major crop failures and famines. The lustre of Nabadwip as a centre of learning and devotional practices only helped to make the choice comparatively easy. A secondary, yet important, consideration for them has been the presence of a tight-knit group of upper-caste Bengalis who, like them, are practising Vaishnavs – devotees of the god Vishnu, whom they also worship as Hari and Krishna. Coming all the way from Sylhet, the family has found a spiritual home with this community. In Sylhet, Hindus have been subjected to a significant degree of enforced conversion to Islam because of the edicts of the local ruler. In Nabadwip, the Vaishnavs feel relatively safe from that. What they do find dismaying is the excessive attachment to power and wealth they see being displayed by many upper-class, wealthy Brahmins. They also feel that the argumentative intricacy of the latest version of scholarly disciplines championed by these elite Brahmins is far removed from the humane aspects of learning. An obsession with the minutiae of reasoning might be intellectually dazzling, but it downplays the fundamental element of spirituality – bhakti, an all-encompassing, self-forgetful love for the divine. The Vaishnavs believe that without bhakti, there is no spiritual fulfilment, no communication with god, and this philosophy sets them apart from the more traditional Hindu Brahmins. It is only natural for them to gravitate towards other like-minded Vaishnav believers and support each other.

~

Temple bells and Sanskrit chants are not the sole expressions of faith in Nabadwip. In the late twelfth century, Bakhtiar Khilji, a Turkic warrior from Afghanistan, invaded Bengal and established his stronghold over an extended territory. By the time of Nimai's birth, large parts of northern and eastern India have come under Muslim rule. In Nabadwip, minarets of mosques compete with temple spires in the skyline, and the Muslim call to prayer is heard loud and clear alongside the sounds of Hindu worship. In the two centuries following Bakhtiar Khilji's arrival, the region has seen the rule of successive Muslim dynasties, many of whose rulers took power through violence. However, despite the agony of bloodshed, loss of property and the large-scale conversion of local Hindus (mostly those from the lower castes) to the faith of their conquerors, Bengal has also benefited from the wisdom of a few exceptional rulers who realized the importance of transiting from a mode of constant aggression to a peaceful administration. Bengal's prosperity and success in trade have been the outcome of their policies of pragmatic accommodation. These sultans have accomplished their larger goals and strengthened their rule by tapping into the talents of the local population. As a result, many qualified and gifted Hindus have found appropriate roles in the court, the army and the local administrative agencies.

Nimai can therefore be said to have been born at a fortunate juncture of Bengali history when the rulers of a foreign faith, after establishing control through blood and violence, have not only worked out some kind of compromise with indigenous religion and cultural beliefs, but also persuaded their non-Muslim citizens that cooperating is wiser than resisting. By the time he is eight years old, a remarkably accomplished, forward-thinking, liberal Muslim ruler has taken power in Bengal – Alauddin Hussain Shah. Like many previous rulers, Hussain Shah, too, has taken the throne by arranging the death of his predecessor. Yet he will leave his mark on the history of the region not as a bloodthirsty tyrant, but as a singularly thoughtful, tolerant and efficient sultan. During his time, there will be a notable renaissance of Bengali culture, the emergence of a distinctive Hindu–Muslim style in art and architecture, a noticeable degree of freedom for Hindu citizens to practise their faith without interference and the appointment of numerous qualified Hindus to senior posts within his administration. Hussain Shah will die when Nimai is thirty-three, but he will have heard of the inspiring young man whose message of seeking god in a radically simple way is being embraced by large numbers of people. It is not unreasonable to look on the simultaneous emergence of two such remarkable figures – so different, yet so similar in their capacity for unconventional thought and action – as something more than coincidence, rather as an event of historic intent on the part of unknown forces.

At the age of eight, of course, Nimai is completely unaware of the sultan who has taken the throne of Bengal. In his late twenties, however, when his life as a monk is consumed by his mission of motivating all people to seek Krishna with an intensity of love regardless of what is preached by orthodox scholars and priests, an unusual connection will be forged between him and the court of the sultan through two of the latter's many able Hindu advisers and officers. They are brothers, Saraswat Brahmins from southern India, and they are highly regarded by the sultan for their intellect, honesty and hard work. Having hired them, he has given them Islamic titles, although it is unclear whether they have had to convert to Islam in return for these privileges. The older is known as Dabir-i-Khas and the younger is called Sakar Mallik. Their father has also worked for the sultan as his private physician, and the family has been well rewarded for their sincere services. With the money they have earned, they have built a palatial residence. Nothing, in material terms, is wanting in their lives. But all will change and the course of their lives reshaped, once they come into contact with an ardent, youthful monk from Nabadwip who possesses nothing except a voice and words that penetrate deep into the receptive heart.

Still, it is unrealistic to think that the prevailing pattern of peaceful cohabitation and professional cooperation, even under an enlightened ruler like Hussain Shah, has erased all localized conflict between the Hindus and Muslims in Bengal or totally done away with outbursts of aggressive social and religious intolerance. From time to time, the surface calm of a prosperous region is also rippled by disturbing undercurrents because of the cross-border raids against the Hindu ruler of neighbouring Orissa carried out by the sultan in an attempt to expand his domain.

Considering the length of the Muslim presence in India, starting with the first invaders who entered the north-western reaches of the land through Afghanistan in the tenth and eleventh centuries and made Delhi their capital, to the later conquests by Bakhtiar Khilji and others that made Hindu Bengal a Muslim sultanate, it seems that Islamic rule is meant to last forever. The Muslim invaders, although they came from different dynasties and had to contend with fierce inter-family power struggles, have been remarkably successful in conquering and retaining territory. Hussain Shah's kingdom may be in the far eastern reaches of India, but his ambition still prompts him to try to expand his boundaries southward to Orissa. Clearly, he does not believe that Muslim rule is likely to cease any time soon. As a result, in Bengal, and in other parts of eastern India, there is a sense of living through an unstable truce which neither Hindu nor Muslim can foresee ending.

~

Nobody, neither scholars in Nabadwip, nor courtiers in Gaur, nor ambitious landowners, prosperous traders or humble peasants, can imagine that a new and unlooked for factor is about to reshape the destiny of the land. Nimai has been born on the cusp of a historic metamorphosis in more senses than one. On 20 May 1498, twelve years after his birth, a Portuguese adventurer will land on India's Malabar coast, far from Nabadwip. Vasco da Gama's arrival will signal the beginning of a European presence that will last for almost five centuries. In 1521, a mere two years after Hussain Shah's death in 1519, the Portuguese will send a mission from western India to the Bengali port of Chittagong, hoping to establish diplomatic ties with the ruler of Bengal.

At this juncture of the fifteenth and sixteenth centuries, the Portuguese, followed by other European races, are about to find a foothold in this vast country and engineer a momentous transformation. The process will be slow and gradual, with short intervals of military violence. But the new ideas, new techniques, new products and new foods that they are bringing with them will be as effective as any conquest by war. They will permanently remould many aspects of Indian life – domestic, social and political – over the next five centuries.

Nimai's mother, Shachi, who is renowned for the way she prepares banana blossom, has not heard of a tuber called the potato which the Portuguese are bringing from a new continent. Nor has she ever seen a fruit called the chilli pepper that adds heat to food. But for future generations of Bengali wives, mothers and cooks, both the potato and the chilli pepper will become the mainstays of the kitchen. When they make banana blossom, they will incorporate these items into the dish to produce a somewhat different preparation from the one that the child Nimai is growing up to love.

# 3

# Boy and Man

The afternoon sun is riding high and the abbreviated shadows cast by trees and houses provide little respite from heat for pedestrians. Even the ghats of the Ganga are deserted. It is time for the town residents to eat lunch and have a restful nap before resuming their daily activities. A boy, about five years old, makes his way along a narrow lane to a school run by the renowned Vaishnav scholar Advaita Acharya, who tutors pupils about Vedanta and the philosophy of bhakti. It is hard to tell if the child has already had his daily bath, since he is covered with the dust and sweat of the playground from where his mother has summoned him to go and fetch his older brother home for lunch. It is a short distance to the school and she knows the boy can safely go by himself. The older brother, immersed in his studies, looks up with a smile when the child comes up to him and tugs at his clothes. He closes his books, gets up and leaves the schoolroom, holding his brother's hand. As the two make their way back home, there is no mistaking the young boy's adoration of his brother and the latter's responsive affection. Together they enter the home where their mother is waiting with the meal she has cooked. They know it will be delicious. Whatever Shachi cooks tastes ambrosial. As they sit down after washing their hands, she serves their lunch – long-grained rice, aubergine seasoned with bitter neem leaves, deep-fried patol, sautéed greens and the boys' favourite, spiced banana blossom with coconut chips and brown chickpeas. Around these items she has put on each plate wedges of lime and pieces of ginger, both meant to aid digestion. And to finish the meal, there is yogurt and milk sweetened with date palm sugar that the region is famed for. As they eat, Shachi looks at her sons with a tender smile – Nimai and Biswarup, her two treasures, her world. She prays every day for their health and happiness.

Nimai, however, is not the quiet, obedient child a parent finds easy to rear. Unlike his meditative, scholarly brother, he is wayward and undisciplined, and as he grows older, he is only too ready to gang up with other neighbourhood children and engage in mischief. He is also prone to tantrums when his elders try to discipline him. The only person he listens to is his brother, but Biswarup, already captivated by the ideals of detachment and abstinence, spends most of his time immersed in books. He is not able to supervise his little brother and keep him out of trouble. Their father, Jagannath Misra, is renowned for his erudition, but he is kept more than busy tutoring his students and performing his priestly duties in order to adequately provide for his family. After his younger son's hatey khori ceremony, which signals the beginning of literacy, Misra has enrolled Nimai in a primary school run by two well-known tutors. But a child's lessons are brief and leave him plenty of time for less desirable activities. Although his intelligence is indisputable, Nimai doesn't show the faintest indication of the scholarly temperament that distinguishes his father and brother. Still, the parents hope that over time he will calm down and learn to comport himself as the son of an eminent Brahmin scholar should.

Life for the Misra family is only moderately comfortable. Given the repeated natural disasters like famine and floods that had beset his native Sylhet, Jagannath Misra does not regret his decision to move to Nabadwip. But a scholar and a teacher can only earn so much. He is thankful that his parents and brother are still in Sylhet and can look after his share of the family property. In good years, some supplemental income accrues from it. He is even more thankful for the human solace and spiritual uplift he finds in the company of his fellow Vaishnavs. The leader of this group is Advaita Acharya, whose reputation as a teacher and philosopher has given him special status. Another prominent member is Sribas, a prosperous Brahmin. The Vaishnavs get together in either of their houses and discuss matters ranging from the nature of bhakti, or selfless devotion, to the pitfalls of excessive worldly attachment and the deplorable values espoused by certain segments of society. Often they pray for a new incarnation of Vishnu to appear and save the world. Occasionally, they sing devotional songs describing the doings of their lord during his last earthly incarnation as Krishna and chant his names. Some get so carried away by their spiritual exhilaration, they laugh and weep loudly, and roll about on the floor in a frenzied fashion. Many of their non-Vaishnav neighbours find such behaviour ridiculous, a disturbance of peace. They even complain to the authorities about it. Nimai and Biswarup don't participate in these emotional musical sessions, but the sound of the melodies is integrated into their consciousness along with the daily clamour of urban life.

~

One day, out of the blue, disaster strikes the family. Biswarup leaves home without telling anyone. The parents discover he has renounced the world and become a monk. Possibly to ensure that his family doesn't try to pressure him into coming back, he has left Nabadwip for an unknown destination. Some of their friends speculate he may have gone to Puri in Orissa where their beloved god is worshipped in the great temple as Jagannath, lord of the universe. Others think he may have travelled south, to the Deccan region, in search of Vaishnav scholars whose philosophy may differ in some aspects from that of Bengali Vaishnavs. His mother secretly blames his teacher, Advaita Acharya, for inspiring him to make this move. Heartbroken, both Shachi and her husband decide that they will not send Nimai to school any more, in case he too gets similar ideas from teachers and classmates. More than anything now, they want to keep their one remaining son at home, even if it means he will grow up as an ignoramus.

It is not a wise decision. Nimai, too, has been devastated at the sudden disappearance of his adored brother and, for a while, he shows no interest in his former activities, preferring to quietly stay home with his parents. But the phase doesn't last. Not having the routine of going to school every day, he falls back into his old habits with a vengeance. Escaping from home, he wanders the streets and often gets into fights with other children. At times, his rowdiness edges into wildness. He invades the homes of his neighbours, enters their kitchens without washing up and grabs whatever food takes his fancy, contaminating the dishes by dipping his fingers into them. If anyone tries to stop him, he shouts at them angrily and throws things around, breaking earthen pots and upsetting the containers and ingredients that have been carefully segregated for purposes of ritual purity. Sometimes, early in the evening, he and his friends wrap themselves in dark blankets and sneak into one or the other of the banana groves surrounding the homes of affluent residents and wreak havoc. When they are satisfied with their rampage, they leave the groves with young plants uprooted and the fruits tossed about, consumed or stolen. Jagannath Misra's only son, people say, is a holy terror. Eventually, the property owners and other townspeople band together and demand that Misra discipline his son and put an end to this obstreperous behaviour.

Reluctantly, Nimai's parents conclude that keeping a nine-year-old boy away from school is doing more harm than good. They enrol him again and hope for improvement. If they had expected a rapid change in behaviour, they are disappointed. Nimai continues to argue and fight with classmates like Murari Gupta and Mukunda Datta. But gradually, he also develops an interest in his studies. Although they don't know it, Murari Gupta will one day write the only credible contemporary account of Nimai's schooldays and youth which other biographers will draw on.

Fate, however, has more suffering in store for this family. The sudden, unexpected death of Jagannath Misra leaves mother and son desolate and facing penury. From being a wilful, self-indulgent youth, Nimai suddenly finds he has to take on the responsibility of being a provider – a role that the teenager is singularly unfit for and unwilling to assume. Instead, he continues to behave in his usual fashion, often making unreasonable demands of his poor mother. When she can't meet them, he explodes with fury. One day he is so enraged that he flings a piece of pottery at her, wounding her forehead. Perhaps this is a turning point. How can a son, even one who is as spoiled and wayward as Nimai, endure the sight of his mother's bleeding face and not be overcome with remorse? Knowing, as he surely does in the depths of his heart, that he is the love of her life, the light of her soul, he has to step away from the moody self-indulgence which has characterized him up to now. He begs her to forgive him and promises to mend his ways. Summoning all his resolve, he starts focusing on his studies, determined to acquire the ability to make a modest living, even if he cannot become as renowned a scholar as his father. His tutors respond with satisfaction, his relatives with relief and his mother with hope and joy.

The inevitable follows. Shachi, confident that her son will now be able to provide for a family, urges him to marry and settle down, despite his youth. She asks her relatives and friends to look for a suitable girl, and they don't have to look far. Lakshmi, the beautiful daughter of the scholar Ballabhacharya, is well known to them. More important, Nimai has occasionally seen her on the river's ghats and is attracted to her. Some say the two have even got to know each other a little. What more natural than the union of such a pair, even if the groom is sixteen and the bride is, at most, thirteen? For Shachi, the wedding symbolizes the beginning of a new life in which her son has become a responsible adult, and she, the elderly widow, can rely on a young woman to help her with all the domestic tasks that are getting to be too much for her.

Soon after, we see Nimai in a new guise. He has become a teacher and tutors young boys in the same school where he used to study. If things had been different, he might have spent a few more years as a student himself, diving into the ancient intricacies of nyaya, tantra and smriti. Perhaps there is a lingering resentment inside him at being thrust prematurely into the role of sole breadwinner. Perhaps he regrets not being considered as accomplished a scholar as his father and brother. Perhaps that is why, even though he has given up the wild behaviour of his childhood, he still cannot resist behaving arrogantly with his contemporaries and elders. He often engages in pointless argument, trying to prove the superiority of his intellect. Once again, his father's friends and other well-wishers express concern at his behaviour. Humility, they say, is a necessary attribute of a great scholar, especially a Vaishnav scholar. Nimai does not pay much heed to this good advice.

~

And then he provides new cause for worry to his family and friends. He starts having strange fits of fainting, shouting and laughing. Sometimes he strikes out wildly at people, at other times he stands frozen, immobile. Occasionally, he can be seen running through the town, loudly proclaiming, 'I am he.' Who is this 'he', people wonder. When he recovers from these episodes, Nimai resumes his daily routine, until the next spell comes over him. Some people believe he is possessed by an evil spirit; others think it is some kind of systemic inflammation. Physicians recommend massaging his head with medicated oil. The episodes don't completely cease, but Nimai is able to continue the semblance of a normal life with a daily routine. After spending the morning with his students, he goes to the Ganga for his bath and comes home for lunch. In the afternoons, refreshed by a siesta, he goes out, wandering about town. Often he makes his way into the market, where weavers, perfumers and dairymen have set up shop along with retailers selling conch shell jewellery, flower garlands and betel leaves. He talks to them without any of the arrogance he displays to his peers, but sometimes behaves like the child he used to be, asking for items he can't pay for. They tolerate him because of his youth, good looks and sweetness of manner.

~

Four years after his father's death, Nimai decides to make a trip to East Bengal, all the way to Sylhet, where his family came from. He plans the journey carefully. The river will be the preferred route, as it was for his parents and others who migrated to Nabadwip, and the trip will be time-consuming. Like his father and other relatives, he too will embark from Nabadwip and travel down the Ganga until it branches out into the Jalangi and, eventually, turns eastward to meet the majestic Padma of eastern Bengal. As it was for them, the final part of his journey to his home town of Dhaka Dakhhin will require him to navigate the enormous lakes and wetlands, which, from a distance, look like miniature oceans. Nimai will be absent from home for quite a while. His mother and his wife worry about possible dangers, but he reassures them. He is convinced the trip will be worth it despite all hardships. He plans to visit educational institutions in the places where he will make stops and he looks forward to meeting scholars with whom he can engage in debate. There is still this need inside him to demonstrate his intellectual prowess and burnish his reputation. He thinks he can do it with people who have never met him and don't know anything about his wild behaviour in childhood and early teens. More important, he plans to meet his paternal family and, with their help, dispose of the landed property he has inherited from his father. This much-needed injection of resources will make his life in Nabadwip more secure. It is an argument that Shachi cannot refute.

When he finally returns home after an absence of three months, he not only brings the money from the sale of property, he is also loaded with valuable gifts from relatives and admirers. One in particular, Tapan Misra, has forged a warm friendship with Nimai even in the short time they have spent together. Although they don't know it now, he and Nimai will again meet some years later, in the holy city of Kashi (Varanasi). In Nabadwip, Nimai disembarks on the familiar, beloved ghat of the Ganga, and makes his way home. He expects a rapturous welcome from his mother and his wife and looks forward to giving them all the fine gifts he has acquired. But what is this? A dark and desolate house confronts him. There is no sign of life, no aroma of appetizing food floating out of the kitchen. Heart pounding with fear and anxiety, Nimai goes inside and finds Shachi lying down, stricken with grief. Tearfully, she informs her son that Lakshmi, his beautiful young wife, has died of snakebite. The triumphant homecoming, the expectations of joyful reunion – all lie in ashes around his feet. Brother, father, beloved young wife – fate has robbed him of each in a cruel and untimely fashion. Life seems almost meaningless.

But he is no longer a tantrum-throwing, spoiled child. After the initial shock, he summons his resolve and resumes his life as a teacher so that he can support himself and his mother. His former waywardness does manifest itself occasionally, when he singles out people from East Bengal – the region he has just visited – and makes fun of them, mimicking their dialects and habits. But on the whole, it is undeniable that his misfortunes have made him draw on his inner strength.

As time goes on, the claims of domesticity

resurrect themselves. A young man must have a wife. And a man cannot mourn for a lifetime. After a suitable interval, Shachi persuades her son to remarry. An appropriate match is found in Bishnupriya, the daughter of a wealthy Brahmin scholar named Sanatan. A family friend, Buddhimanta Khan, covers the cost of a resplendent wedding. Everyone hopes that from now on fate will be kind, that Shachi's beloved son, her one remaining treasure, will no longer be subjected to unforeseen trials.

~

This may be the time to take a good look at Nimai. He is still very young, though he lives in a time and place where life can be short and adulthood is thrust upon one fairly early. He has experienced repeated tragedy, but he has decided not to abandon hopes for a second chance at contentment and comfort. Lakshmi was a dearly beloved wife and he may have enshrined her in his heart, but to all appearances, he is content with his new marriage, his ability to support his mother and wife, and the friendships he has cultivated.

His good looks are remarkable. Everyone is struck by this tall, fair-skinned young man with graceful posture, handsome features, beautiful, elongated eyes and a head of abundant, wavy black hair. He is not immune to vanity either. He takes great care of his appearance, wearing dhotis with beautiful borders, anointing his hair with scented oil and perfuming his body with sandalwood and musk. On occasion, he buys flower garlands and wears them round his neck or twines them in his hair. When he walks the streets of Nabadwip, heads turn, and those who do not know him ask who he is. It is Nimai, they are told, son of the late Vaishnav scholar Jagannath Misra and his wife Shachi, Nimai, who has survived the tragic assaults of fate, whose golden beauty inspires the moniker of Gora and Gouranga. Neither Nimai nor anybody else in Nabadwip is aware that he is standing on the edge of an extraordinary metamorphosis.

# 4

# Epiphany and Transition

Behind the placid routine of life at home, however, Nimai is still mourning the loss of his father and his first wife. He is filled with anguish whenever he thinks of how Lakshmi must have suffered from the effects of the snake venom raging in her body. Unnatural deaths like these are supposed to affect the soul's passage to the next world. After some months, Nimai decides to make another journey – this time to the town of Gaya, one of Hinduism's holiest sites. It is famed for its temples dedicated to Vishnu and there is an ancient belief that making offerings to the dead in Gaya releases the soul from the cycle of rebirth. Departed ancestors who have received such offerings send their blessings to the living.

This time, Nimai will not be travelling alone. He decides to join a group of pilgrims with whom to make the trek to Gaya. His uncle, Chandrashekhar Acharya, also decides to accompany him. The distance is considerable, but the journey is not as onerous as the one he made by himself to East Bengal. On the way, Nimai succumbs once to a bout of fever, but he recovers quickly. Performing the rituals of offering in Gaya brings him solace, a sense of completion, of duty done. No one knows better than Nimai himself what anxiety his father had suffered because of his rambunctious behaviour in childhood and youth, and now he hopes he has made some amends. Watching him go through these rituals, his uncle Chandrashekhar Acharya hopes that after returning to Nabadwip Nimai will be able to settle down to the peaceful routine of being a teacher and a family man.

This, however, is not to be. The unexpected is only waiting round the corner. During a visit to the Vishnu temple where there is a slab of stone in which two enormous footprints – supposedly the footprints of Vishnu himself – are embedded, Nimai is suddenly overcome with a flood of intense emotion. He has an incredible vision that he is unable to describe in words. The impact is simply astounding. He weeps and cries out the name of Krishna, he looks around as if he actually expects to see the beautiful blue-skinned god in these mortal surroundings. His uncle and his fellow pilgrims try to soothe him and bring him back to a sense of reality. Their success is only partial.

Soon after, while he is still in the grasp of this mysterious emotional upheaval, Nimai has one of the most pivotal encounters of his life. He meets the holy man Ishwar Puri, a follower of the legendary Vaishnav practitioner Madhabendra Puri. While everybody else thinks that Nimai's strange emotional outbursts indicate a relapse into the pattern of seizures that affected him in the past, Ishwar Puri interprets his behaviour as a manifestation of something spiritual and otherworldly. With great tenderness, he takes Nimai under his wing and initiates him into the direct path of Vaishnav spiritualism by teaching him the Gopal Mantra. Nimai's fellow travellers, as they make ready to return to Nabadwip, hope that the beneficial effects of the mantra will reduce his seizures. For now they cannot imagine that within a short time this high-strung, emotional young man will be transformed into the leader of a spiritual movement that will sweep through Bengal and beyond. If Ishwar Puri, observing Nimai's overt and intense yearning for Krishna, has any idea about the future, he does not give any indication.

# 5

# Fellowship and Congregation

Winter is edging into spring when Nimai and his companions return to Nabadwip. His mother and his wife are, as is only to be expected, relieved and happy that he has come back home safely. However, it is the town's small Vaishnav community that is in for a joyful surprise. For Nimai no longer keeps his distance from them. He wholeheartedly joins their gatherings, participating in discussions and devotional music and making no secret of his new obsessive longing for Krishna. What is even more astonishing is the change in his persona. Where, they wonder, is the arrogant, self-assured young man who was so eager to demonstrate his superiority over well-known scholars, who plunged into arguments with his contemporaries, who never hesitated to ridicule those he considered his inferior? In his place, they are confronted with a totally different man, a personification of the modesty, humility and introspection that are the ideals of Vaishnav conduct. When he expresses his love and longing for Krishna, he displays a depth of emotion that astonishes contemporaries like Murari Gupta, Mukunda Datta and Gadadhar Misra, as well as elders of the community like Sribas and Chandrashekhar Acharya and even the venerable academic Advaita Acharya.

Their joy, however, finds no echoes in Nimai's household. Although he has resumed taking classes, the unpredictability of his behaviour has not disappeared. He finds it hard to concentrate on the subjects he teaches and students find it more and more difficult to learn from him. When he is not giving tutorials, he is frequently overcome by the same old seizure-like symptoms that used to bedevil him before his trip to Gaya – only their intensity is magnified. He laughs, he cries, he shouts, he even roars at people. He hardly ever sleeps. His wife runs away from him in terror. As is only to be expected, the parents of his pupils withdraw their children from Nimai's little school. He is left with no work or regular source of income.

The community, however, gathers around to support him. In fact, they are enthralled to find him in their midst and feel an unexpected elation whenever he is with them. They get together every evening, either in Nimai's home or, when the gathering is big, in the spacious homes of prosperous citizens like Sribas. They talk about the philosophy of bhakti which, they agree, triumphs over all other means of attaining god. They debate how best an individual can embrace humility and tolerance in daily conduct and integrate bhakti in his or her consciousness while going through domestic and professional life. And they raise their voices in joyful unison to sing devotional kirtans about Krishna or chant the supreme mantra honouring him – Hare Krishna Hare Krishna / Krishna Krishna Hare Hare / Hare Rama Hare Rama / Rama Rama Hare Hare.

At one point, the venerable teacher and scholar Advaita Acharya decides to move from Nabadwip to the neighbouring town of Shantipur. When he comes to say goodbye to the group, he is suddenly overcome with a vision of Nimai as the embodiment of Krishna himself. He gives Nimai the same ritual offerings he uses in worship and touches the young man's feet with reverence. This incident further energizes the Vaishnav community's allegiance to Nimai.

Although singing and chanting are not new for them, Nimai's unspoken leadership bands them into a holy congregation. They have already internalized the idea that communal singing is a way of worship as valid as any age-old ritualistic tradition involving priests, prayers and offerings. Watching Nimai singing and dancing, they also recognize its potential as the means to draw more people into the fold. The older and more experienced among them, however, do not indulge in unrealistic expectations, being fully aware of how careful they have to be in spreading their message at this nascent stage of their movement. They recognize that people who are adamantly orthodox and still hew to the ancient Brahminical ways of worship will do their best to sabotage the Vaishnavs' efforts by publicly deriding them. So they ensure that such people are kept far from their gatherings. Not that it stops non-believers from ridiculing the Vaishnavs for what they consider bizarre and self-indulgent displays of physicality and intense emotion. They laugh at those who, like Nimai, fall into trances and fits and burst into sudden bouts of tears. To these sceptics, Nimai is little better than a lunatic leading a pack of lunatics. Then there are the alarmists, who harp on the public's fear that the Vaishnavs' uninhibited acts of communal religiosity will arouse the hostility of the authorities. After all, they are living in a land that is ruled by Muslims. Even if the sultan himself is not intolerant, there is no dearth of low-ranking Muslim officials who can take umbrage at the actions of this segment of the Hindu populace and respond by penalizing everyone.

The Vaishnavs respond to such fear-mongering with calm and confident enthusiasm. Their numbers may be small, but their faith in the future is unshakeable. The new members of the group look to the long-time stalwarts who have remained steadfast through the years and given strength to those who falter. One of the most remarkable members of the group is a Muslim by birth who has chosen to become a Vaishnav – an unusual example of conversion to a religion where conversion is not a tradition. Later, historians will refer to him as Jaban Haridas. Born in the Jessore district of eastern Bengal, Haridas is an exemplary believer, for he has endured much oppression from his fellow Muslims who feel betrayed by him. After moving from place to place in search of safety and shelter, he has finally come to settle in Nabadwip where Advaita Acharya has given him much support. His conduct is that of a model Vaishnav. Living with utmost simplicity, he occupies himself by chanting Krishna's name three hundred thousand times a day. When Nimai gets to know him, he is overwhelmed with affection for this unassuming, devoted man who has not lost his serenity and tolerance in spite of all his tribulations.

As word spreads, more and more Vaishnav devotees from distant parts of Bengal come to Nabadwip to meet the charismatic new leader. There is an electric charge in the air when they gather for singing and chanting with Nimai. Moreover, they discover with delight that although he had been a wild and unmanageable child and frequently displayed wilful obstreperousness in his early youth, he has also somehow managed to become an accomplished singer and dancer. He has probably acquired these skills from watching the jatra performances by troupes of actors who travel from town to town, village to village, throughout Bengal. This expertise, combined with an inborn grace and depth of feeling, makes Nimai a star performer in the Vaishnav community's theatrical performances.

Increasingly, these performances take place in the homes of affluent Vaishnavs, where the community gathers to watch and discover how gifted a thespian Nimai is. The plays are always based on the events of Krishna's life as depicted in myths and literature. As is customary, male actors play the parts of both men and women, but Nimai's versatility is particularly evident whenever he takes on a female role. The verisimilitude he projects is quite astonishing – his body robed in a sari, his feet tinted with a vermilion solution, his ankles showing off the musical dancing bells tied around them, his handsome features adorned with make-up to create the image of an entrancing woman. His mother and wife occasionally come to watch these performances, and on one occasion even Shachi is fooled by his female guise and fails to recognize her son.

~

A new and striking figure arrives in Nabadwip around this time, injecting a burst of fresh energy into the town's Vaishnav community. Nityananda (sometimes called Nityananda Abadhoot), born in the western Bengal district of Birbhum, is a man who has already travelled far and wide. Initially, many of the Vaishnavs he meets find him both enigmatic and intriguing. Dressed in dark-blue clothing, he carries a staff and a spouted water jug with a handle – all of which are the traditional symbols of a worshipper of Shiva, not Vishnu. His personality and manner can be jarring at times. He displays little or no regard for conventions and often dresses in a flamboyant style. In certain moods, he can even disrobe in public, without embarrassment. Nor is he averse to drinking alcohol. As for the centuries-old traditions of Hindu society, especially the rigidity of the caste system promoted by Brahmins, he has absolutely no patience with such practices, despite being a Brahmin by birth.

Before coming to Nabadwip, Nityananda has had an encounter with the renowned Vaishnav spiritualist Madhabendra Puri, who aroused his interest in Vaishnavism even though he was still practising Shaivism. But what has now drawn him to Nabadwip are the numerous stories floating around about a resurgent Vaishnav movement under a charismatic young leader who espouses bhakti above all else. Before coming to Nabadwip he had met Advaita Acharya in Shantipur and was very impressed with his scholarship and spirituality. Now his encounter with Nimai has an even deeper spiritual impact. He moves away from the practice of Shaivism (which is less prevalent in Bengal than in other parts of India) and becomes a Vaishnav. In a formal gesture of transition, he discards his dark clothes and breaks the staff and water pot he has been travelling with. Very soon, a close bond develops between this energetic newcomer and young Nimai. Nityananda is ten or twelve years older, which is probably one of the reasons why both Nimai and Shachi see in him a semblance to the long-lost Biswarup. People notice the affection that Nityananda has aroused in mother and son and start calling him Nitai, to rhyme with Nimai, as if they are indeed two brothers.

~

And Nimai realizes that he has found a most able lieutenant to help spread his message. Along with Haridas and several others, Nimai forms the core group that will take the faith to the public arena. They will not wait for new followers to come to them. Instead, they will take their communal chanting and singing into the streets of Nabadwip. Religious music, heard in the confines of the home, will now be heard from street to street, square to square. Sceptic and believer alike will be amazed at this new way of helping ordinary people reach god. Singing and chanting in unison, kirtan will become sankirtan, a collective, congregational enterprise.

Fear and embarrassment are cast by the wayside. Even the most reticent members of the group show a surprising willingness to sing and dance in front of the townsfolk so that Nimai's message can reach far and wide. Nor are all the people joining Nimai members of the lower castes. Many Brahmins and members of the upper castes have by now chosen to shake off the ossified doctrines that have ruled their lives and found liberation in Nimai's call to take the path of bhakti. They have come to believe that once others hear what Nimai has been saying – that Krishna may be a god, but he is accessible to all, that he does not have to be placated with arcane rituals and expensive offerings made through Brahmin priests, that merely chanting his name with full-throated love and heartfelt devotion will bring him close to us, that his love is given equally to the lowest of the low, to the poorest of the poor, to the downtrodden untouchable and the Muslim heathen – they cannot but be moved. It is, however, a revolutionary message, and it carries its own dangers, as Nimai and his cohorts are about to discover.

The evening hours in Nabadwip are transformed. Until now, it is the blowing of conch shells, the ringing of bells, the incantations of priests performing evening worship in the temples, the conversation of townspeople, the commercial exchanges in the market, the lapping of the Ganga against the ghats that have constituted the town's soundscape. Nimai and the Vaishnavs add a radical new note as they form a procession and set out loudly chanting the Hare Krishna mantra set to the tune of evening ragas and accompanied by the sweet rhythm of the khol and the silvery beat of the khanjani. As they progress, people stop their usual activities and come to their doors and windows to look. Such a sight has never been seen. Traditionally, communal singing is heard at local fairs when small choral groups perform for public entertainment. For the fairgoers, it is one among many activities to be enjoyed in a fairground. But this – this resounding chorus of voice and instrument – fills the daily living space of the townsfolk. This is no small group singing for a little while. This is a procession that keeps growing as the singers move through streets and neighbourhoods, expressing a raw emotional energy. It feels like a revolution of sorts and it rocks staid, scholarly Nabadwip society to its foundations. Observers react with a mixture of surprise, admiration and antipathy. The Vaishnavs hope that eventually the positive feelings will outweigh the negative.

As true believers, they remind themselves that humility, love and tolerance will always triumph over prejudice and hatred.

And one evening, their belief is put to the test. The community has heard of two men, Jagai and Madhai, who have been terrorizing a particular neighbourhood. Unlike most thugs, neither are they uneducated nor do they belong to the lower rungs of the caste order. They have employment as town guards. Brahmins by birth, they act like complete ruffians, indulging in forbidden foods like beef and drinking to the point of intoxication. They take pleasure in harassing innocent passers-by and react violently whenever anyone objects to their behaviour. Nityananda and Haridas decide they will confront these two sinners and convert them to the peaceful way of Vaishnavism. Their initial attempt fails miserably. The men attack them with such violence that they barely escape with their lives. Tormented by this failure, Nityananda decides to risk approaching the men again, alone. This time he gets hit by a piece of broken pottery that makes his forehead bleed. Even as he retreats, he makes a statement of forgiveness that will echo down the ages: 'You may have hit me with a potsherd, but that hasn't stopped my desire to give you my love.'

When Nimai hears of this incident, his reaction is not quite as mild as one would expect from a Vaishnav leader. Rounding up many of his followers, he goes and confronts Jagai and Madhai. Whether it is because of the large number of people facing them or because of some extraordinary aura projected by Nimai, they cringe with fear and beg to be forgiven. Nimai is only too glad to accept their change of heart. He knows that in the future these unlikely converts will become exemplary Vaishnavs who will inspire many others to join the fold.

Confronting two drunken miscreants, though, is a relatively small matter. Very soon the Vaishnavs are faced with a much bigger problem. As more and more people join their evening processions, opposition grows among both the orthodox coterie of Hindu society and the Muslims of Nabadwip. Some of them complain to Muslim judges and administrators about the Vaishnavs disturbing the peace. One evening in Simulia, a part of town where most residents are Muslims, the inevitable happens. The two sides confront each other, heated arguments lead to violence and Nimai's followers act in a most un-Vaishnav way, damaging property, destroying gardens, perhaps even assaulting their opponents, who respond with equal force, returning blow for blow, some breaking the singers' instruments. Eventually, a Muslim official, aware that such intercommunity confrontation has to be stopped before it gets out of hand, negotiates with both parties to arrive at a peaceful resolution. It is an incident full of dramatic potential and it will be embellished with every retelling until it acquires the dimensions of an epic clash and a crushing defeat for the Muslim residents and their lawmakers. It is also the kind of incident that can stoke the fires of continuing resentment among ordinary Muslims in the Nabadwip area. What neither Nimai nor his Muslim critics yet know is that one day even the great sultan of Bengal, Hussain Shah, will become one of his admirers. Well aware of the tendency of low-level officials to harass Hindu religious leaders whose growing influence they might consider a threat, the sultan has already made it an official policy to penalize such antisocial violence. Later, as he gets to hear more about Nimai, the sultan will come to look on him as a figure who commands deep admiration and respect, regardless of what message he preaches.

~

Meanwhile, among the Vaishnavs, Nimai's image as a man whose intense spirituality coexists with a fearless dedication to liberate people from the chains of clerical orthodoxy continues to grow. Although he has taken part in this showdown with a section of the town's Muslims, his followers are always happy to point out that he has no personal prejudice against them. His embrace of Haridas is a prime example of his independent, generous thinking. At one point, Chaitanya even declared Haridas to be spiritually superior. 'Your touch purifies me,' he said. 'Your dedication to learning the scriptures, to meditate with devotion, to make many pilgrimages – all make you a person holier than many Brahmins.' Extraordinary praise, indeed, for a man who was born a Muslim. Chaitanya's reputation as an iconoclast is further reinforced when he flouts one of the cardinal laws of Hindu society – that a high-caste person who consumes food or water touched by those who are consigned to the untouchable category immediately becomes an outcaste. Such a person's family, too, is put beyond the pale and his peers refuse to socialize or eat with him. Because of this, even Vaishnavs who have discarded many of the age-old shibboleths of Hindu society do not care to cross this line. Recovering one's caste status can only be done after performing harsh rituals of purification.

Nimai, however, Brahmin though he is, and willing to respect his fellow Brahmins' social practices, is not cowed by the spectre of ritual penalty being imposed on him. Parched with thirst on a hot day, he happens to walk past the house of Sridhar, a humble member of a lower caste who makes a living by selling vegetables. Nimai knows Sridhar quite well. As a mischievous child, he would often scatter the vegetables Sridhar had made ready to take to market. This day, he sees a pitcher of water on Sridhar's porch and stops to drink from it. His companions, perhaps even Sridhar himself, urge him not to, fearful of the upper-caste elite ostracizing him, but Nimai brushes away their objections. Having discarded the orthodoxies of life and worship, he explains, he no longer cares about ritual penalties being imposed on him. Pouring some water from the pitcher, he washes his face and hands and drinks his fill. Secretly, perhaps, he also hopes that this rebellious act will further encourage his followers to muster up the courage to fight against long-standing prohibitions.

~

Although he has become the unquestioned leader of the Vaishnav community and spends most of his time with them, Nimai still remains a bit of an enigma. Even his closest friends and acolytes are not necessarily privy to his innermost thoughts and feelings. Many of his unconventional doings have taken them by surprise and some of them are still not sure about the wisdom of every one of his actions. Even his mother Shachi, who has known him the longest, cannot read him with confidence. His strange fits and trances, his bouts of weeping, his ecstatic chanting followed by joyous dancing followed by frenzied movements, his boldness in going out on the streets with his followers even if it provokes a large segment of the town residents – what do they all add up to? Even his decision to engage wholeheartedly in the communal practice of Vaishnavism after his return from Gaya is still not fully understood. His life at home is unlike that of any householder or Brahmin scholar. He has a beautiful, dutiful wife, yet he does not spend time with her. He is surrounded by loving relatives and friends, yet a part of him remains shrouded and inaccessible to them.

And from this indecipherable interior emerges yet another decision that shatters whatever peace Shachi had till now. Nimai decides to give up the life of the householder and become a monk. He informs Nityananda and Mukunda and Gadadhar of his decision before telling some of the others. He informs them about his plan to go to Katwa, which is on the other side of the Ganga, and take his vow of sanyas or renunciation from Keshab Bharati, a member of the ancient renunciation order founded by Shankara, the eighth-century Hindu religious reformer. There has been some talk that Nimai's brother Biswarup also took orders from a member of this sect. One can imagine the heartbreak that afflicts Shachi as her long-held anxiety is justified.

She is about to lose her only remaining child. The path taken by Biswarup is now to be followed by Nimai. And what of Nimai's wife Bishnupriya? She is the most unseen presence in his life. As a dutiful, traditional Hindu wife, she has always served him at home, helped her mother-in-law with domestic chores, longed for intimacy with her sweet-natured husband, even hoped for a family. None of her desires have been fulfilled and now she is faced with a permanent loss. She will be a single woman despite being married, as good as a widow. She will never be a mother. The only way for her to be connected to her husband will be as a devotee, not a spouse or companion. Does Nimai care at all? No one knows.

In the earliest predawn darkness, Nimai leaves home with five trusted companions and arrives in Katwa. The next day, the third of February 1510, he is inducted into monkhood by Keshab Bharati. In the time-honoured gesture of rejecting worldly vanity, Nimai's beautiful black locks are shorn, exposing his bare skull. His clothes, too, are discarded and replaced with the simple saffron garb of the holy mendicant. This is a radically different makeover from the upanayan or sacred thread ceremony he underwent as a young boy, the ceremony that signals the second birth of a Brahmin. At that time, too, his hair had been shaved off, and he had undertaken an ascetic life for a prescribed number of days, wearing simple clothes, carrying a walking stick and asking for charity. But that was a temporary ceremonial phase. Seeing him then, his parents had only shed tears of joy, watching their child reach the first stage of adulthood. This morning in Katwa though, had Shachi been present, her tears would have turned into a river as she watched her son permanently turn away from the bonds of domestic life.

After the formal induction, Keshab Bharati gives Nimai a new name for his new life – Krishna Chaitanya, the consciousness of Krishna. Mostly, from now on, people will refer to him as Chaitanya. Twenty-three years, eleven months and six days after the fateful night of the lunar eclipse, Nimai begins to recede into the land of memory – the recollections of his mother, uncle, teachers, wife and childhood friends. The world is ready for Chaitanya.

# Part Two

# Chaitanya

# 6

# From Home to World

The young sanyasi, newly liberated from the ties of affection, comfort and the security of a predictable life, chooses to do what others have done before him – travel and pilgrimage, which constitute the path to a new life of non-attachment and spiritual seeking. But he has no firm destination in mind yet, nor does that bother him. After all, a sanyasi can be a wandering mendicant without following a fixed travel plan. Having left home for good, Chaitanya has made the world his home, and he can go in whichever direction he pleases, provided he is not distracted from his spiritual quest. Nimai's previous travels in Bengal took him to the eastern parts of the region, where land and water seem to overlap in a blue and green panorama. This time, he is taken with the idea of going to the western Rarh area, a contrasting landscape of harsh brown, arid stretches of land studded with rows of date palm trees, and a red laterite soil that feels stony underfoot and is host to stands of the golden-flowered acacia. He spends a few days there, accompanied by Nityananda and others, before switching direction in the hope of going to Mathura and Brindaban, the legendary sites of Krishna's life on earth. But the journey is onerous and conditions of travel harsh. His companions persuade him to turn back towards Katwa and go down the Ganga till he reaches the next town, Shantipur.

At the river ghat in Shantipur, they are met by the elderly Advaita Acharya, who makes no secret of his affection and veneration for this young monk. To most observers, it is evident that in his heart of hearts Advaita Acharya believes Chaitanya to be an incarnation of Krishna, who had declared in the verses of the Bhagavad Gita that he would always appear on earth when righteousness was under assault, in order to save the virtuous and destroy the evildoers. Now, when Chaitanya appears before him as a young sanyasi, Acharya is not only overwhelmed with delight, his belief in the young monk's divinity is also deeply affirmed. In later years, many other followers will also think the same and worship Chaitanya as a god, but he himself will firmly repudiate the idea, saying, 'Do not think of me as Vishnu or Krishna. I am a mere mortal, not a divine being.'

Chaitanya's mother had once bitterly blamed the old man for inspiring her older son Biswarup to become a monk, but Chaitanya has tried hard to convince her that a person who takes the vows of sanyas does so of his own volition. Whether Acharya is aware of Shachi's former hostility towards him or not, Chaitanya senses no constraint in the old man's offer of hospitality. His own love and respect for this man who has been both teacher and guide to so many Vaishnavs in Nabadwip is as deep as ever.

It is a pleasant interlude. Acharya and his family welcome him with wholehearted joy and veneration and, as word spreads of his presence, many local Vaishnavs come to meet him. This is the first time that a large number of people see Chaitanya not simply as a dedicated leader of the Vaishnav community, but also as a sanyasi who has given up all worldly pleasures to focus on spreading his message to the public. But while he is a guest in the house of an admirer like Acharya, Chaitanya does not have to be deprived of every pleasure. He is not the kind of monk who believes he has to seclude himself in a mountain cave in search of personal salvation and live on a spartan diet of milk and fruits. He has renounced his worldly life so that he can be close to the greater public, be accessible to anyone who wants to find a simple path to god. Austerity for its own sake has no relevance in his mission, particularly because he wants to convey to all that leading a normal domestic life is not necessarily an obstacle to seeking and finding god. So when Advaita Acharya begs him to briefly accept his hospitality and share a meal with his family and friends, Chaitanya sees no reason to refuse. A monk who rejects the offer of food, cooked with loving care and devotion, would inflict the same kind of heartbreak on his disciples as would a god who rejects offerings made by a devotee. And having been a loving son for many years, Chaitanya is undoubtedly reminded of the care with which Shachi used to prepare meals for him and the intense pleasure she derived from serving him, watching him eat and hearing him express appreciation of her cooking. Now he has left his mother forever and deprived her of that happiness, but in the home of a sincere and devoted friend he cannot say no to the offer of sharing a communal meal.

And what a meal it is. Acharya's wife is a great cook, but on this occasion she seems to be guided by superhuman inspiration and energy. In her mind, as in her husband's, there is little doubt that cooking for Chaitanya is the same as cooking for Krishna. The meal is served on a whole banana leaf. In the centre there is a mound of fine white rice – the best of the previous autumn's harvest – tinted yellow by the ghee poured over it. Around the rice are arranged leaf containers of vegetables and moong dal. There are several kinds of greens, as well as preparations of patol, pumpkin and taro. There are root vegetables cooked with black pepper, mustard and dried herbs. There is also one of Chaitanya's favourite items – aubergine fried with new young neem leaves. Does he remember he was called Nimai in his previous life because everyone hoped that the association with bitter neem leaves would keep death at bay? On one corner of the banana leaf there is an arrangement of fried dal pellets, light and airy in texture, together with round slices of pumpkin and taro that have also been fried crisp. And as is only to be expected, there is yet another of his favourite dishes, a preparation of banana blossom. Surely he has a memory of savouring it the way his mother used to make this. These items are followed by several tart concoctions, and finally Chaitanya is served dessert. Not just one item but a plethora of sweets made with coconuts, bananas, ground dal, wheat flour and rice flour. The finishing touch is provided by the food of the gods – rice pudding topped with fragrant ghee.

Although the young monk accepted Acharya's invitation, he had not anticipated the elaborate nature of the banquet. Half-jokingly he says he cannot possibly sit down to such a meal, since a monk is only supposed to eat one simple meal a day and that is all the sustenance he needs. Acharya, of course, does not take no for an answer. Referring to his own conviction that Chaitanya is an incarnation of Krishna, he says that in the temple in Puri where Krishna is worshipped as Jagannath, the priests offer him huge quantities of food three times a day. If there is no objection to that, why should Chaitanya not eat what Acharya's wife has cooked for him? Chaitanya admits he is beaten by this affectionate argument, as indeed Krishna himself once submitted to the gopis in Brindaban because their love for him was so pure. But he cannot be selfish in his indulgence. His faithful followers Haridas and Mukunda, who have been travelling with him, are waiting outside. He demands that they be brought in and seated. It gives him pleasure to personally serve them the delicious food.

~

As expected, the time in Shantipur is spent in philosophical discussions about the nature of bhakti. But there are also many hours of singing, chanting and dancing together with the local Vaishnavs who rejoice in this opportunity to meet Chaitanya. As in Nabadwip, his presence energizes the community here to defend their faith against the assaults of Brahminical orthodoxy and oppressive measures of the Muslim population.

Over the next few weeks, Chaitanya also discusses his plans for the future with those who are most intimate with him. To spread his message, he needs to be in a populated area. But staying in Nabadwip or any other place in Bengal can leave open the possibility of being drawn back into the ties and obligations of familial love and domesticity. After much discussion, he decides that Puri would be the ideal place to live in, for now at least. It is in a neighbouring province and not too far from Nabadwip. Moreover, there is a constant flow of pilgrims who come from all over Bengal to visit the Jagannath temple in Puri. Through them Chaitanya will be able to get news about his mother and she about him. Perhaps Puri also draws him because he has heard that his brother Biswarup went there after he became a monk and eventually died there. Above all, Puri is home to Jagannath, who is Chaitanya's beloved god Krishna in another form.

His friends concur with this decision and after some consultation it is decided that he will be accompanied on this journey by Nityananda, Gadadhar, Mukunda, Damodar, Gobinda and some others. In Puri, there are prominent Vaishnavs who will welcome the group and help them settle in a new place. The eminent scholar

Sarbabhouma Bhattacharya is an influential man. Even Prataparudra, the king of Orissa, admires and respects him. Sarbabhouma's brother-in-law, Gopinath Acharya, also lives in Puri and can look after Chaitanya if need arises.

The moment of parting from the young monk he loves and adores is hard for Advaita Acharya. Chaitanya is also deeply moved. By way of consolation he tells his former teacher how much he cherishes him, that he believes Acharya is one of those superior beings whose heart is 'not only tender as a flower but also potent as a bolt of thunder' and that he will find the strength to endure the pain of this separation.

~

The journey facing Chaitanya and his followers will be an arduous one and they are all prepared for hardship. Given the uneven road conditions, they anticipate taking more than a month to reach Puri. Initially, they plan to travel along the banks of the Ganga, stopping at riverside towns for rest. But after they get to the port of Saptagram, they know that towns and habitations will dwindle in number.

Bengal will show a different, less hospitable face and they will have to pass through large areas of undeveloped wilderness and a fractured river system with numerous canals and tributaries. They will also have to protect themselves from bandits and marauders as they journey through these lawless areas before reaching the border of Orissa. It is also a particularly dangerous time for travelling to Orissa. For the past several years, the sultan of Bengal, Hussain Shah, has been making frequent raids across the border into northern Orissa. In response, King Prataparudra has fought back bravely, but the fortunes of war have been uneven. What Chaitanya and his cohorts do not know is that on some previous occasions the sultan's soldiers have even got as far as Puri and ransacked its environs, destroying Hindu temples and the deities installed in them. Out of fear that the idols in the great Jagannath temple will be desecrated, the priests have sometimes removed them and hidden them under the waters of the enormous Lake Chilika along with all the gold and treasure that have been donated to the temple over the years.

Still, each member of the little group of

travellers is elated at the thought of reaching his destination and the first part of their journey is uneventful. Once they reach the border, they cross the Subarnarekha river and gradually make their way, with brief halts in Remuna, Jajpur and Cuttack, the last being of particular interest to Vaishnav devotees because it is the site of the temple of Sakshigopal, Gopal the Witness. Chaitanya is deeply moved when he sets eyes on the statue of Gopal, a representation of Krishna as a youthful cowherd in Brindaban. His companions are all familiar with the legend associated with this temple, yet Chaitanya insists on recounting it again, for at its core is a concept that is dear to his heart and also a part of his message.

Two Brahmins, one old and frail, the other young and vigorous, set out together from Vidyanagar in southern Orissa for a pilgrimage to Brindaban. During the arduous trek north, the younger man takes the greatest care of his companion, attending to all his needs like a faithful servant, although he is under no obligation to do so. Moved by such selfless behaviour, the older man decides that the only appropriate reward would be to give the young man the hand of his daughter in marriage. The young Brahmin, however, cannot believe that such a thing is at all possible, given the enormous rift of wealth and class that separates him from his fellow pilgrim. Finally, to convince him of the sincerity of his intent, the old man goes to a temple where there is a statue of Gopal and asks the deity to be a witness to his promise. The statue may be stone, but to the faithful, it is alive, and an undertaking given with the statue as a witness is unbreakable. The young man has no option but to believe in the sincerity of his elderly companion and expresses his deepest gratitude. The two complete their pilgrimage and make their way back to Vidyanagar in perfect amity. At home, however, things change. The old man's sons violently repudiate his choice of son-in-law, and he is too weak to stand up to them. Even the villagers agree that it is absurd for the daughter of an eminent and wealthy person to marry a penniless youth even if he is a Brahmin by caste. The young man, angry at such perfidy, even though it is not totally unexpected, makes his way back to the temple of Gopal and asks him to come to Vidyanagar and verify the undertaking given in front of him. It is an absurd request, for the statue of a god cannot become part of human life. But the power of faith overrules all else. Gopal's statue comes to life and he agrees to follow the young Brahmin all the way to Vidyanagar, provided the latter never looks back. Delighted, the young man sets off for home, comforted by the sound of Gopal's ankle bells that chime behind him at every step. Halfway along the route, however, all goes silent. Not realizing that it is because they are walking through a sandy stretch that muffles the chime of the ankle bells, the young man looks back, only to see the image of Gopal become transfixed in the sand. No appeal or prayer can bring him back to life and motion.

But that, Chaitanya delights in pointing out, is not the end of the story. Krishna, in whatever form you worship him, always responds to true devotion. When the young man reaches his village and tells everyone what has happened, the incredulous villagers follow him back to the spot where they see the statue of Gopal standing in the middle of nowhere, far from the temple where it had been originally installed. They realize that the god had indeed kept his promise to be a witness and left his temple to help his devotee, even though the latter's single moment of doubt has again transformed him into an inanimate statue. The rich Brahmin and his sons have no option but to bow before this divine witness and agree to the marriage. A new temple is built around the statue and becomes a famed pilgrimage site. The young Brahmin becomes the officiating priest. For Chaitanya, there is no greater evidence of Krishna's love for the poor and the underprivileged, a love that no amount of wealth and status can buy. This is at the heart of the message that he wants to preach.

~

From Cuttack, Chaitanya and his companions resume their journey. The closer they get to Puri, the more excited they are. Chaitanya is overwhelmed by his mental vision of this ancient city of pilgrimage, which was originally referred to as Jagannathpuri. In his mind and that of his Bengali followers, it is more familiar as Nilachal, the blue mountain, because the great temple of Jagannath was built on a hillock in the centre of a lagoon. The central area of the city is laid out in the shape of a conch shell, evoking Panchajanya, the powerful conch that the god Vishnu carries in one of his four hands. The temple itself is surrounded by rings of various structures – smaller temples, monasteries, cloisters, religious academies, residences of the temple priests and staff. All are held together in the invisible yet eternal outline of the conch which has given Puri yet another name – Shankhakshetra. It is one of the holiest of holies in the Hindu world and all who come here are touched and elevated by its spirituality. And, from a more pragmatic point of view, it is a town that already has a significant Vaishnav population. Once Chaitanya connects with them, once they accept his particular kind of Vaishnavism which elevates bhakti above observance, knowledge and priestly ritual, they are likely to disseminate his ideas to relatives and friends living in other parts of Orissa and even out of the province. Some of Chaitanya's followers also hope that the centuries-entrenched priestly community of the Jagannath temple might also one day be attracted to Chaitanya's message, even if they cannot adopt it. Besides, as Chaitanya has, by now, made clear to them, he does not advocate bhakti as the one and only path to god, exclusive of all ritual and observance. For the son of a Brahmin family, those latter elements have always been part of life and he recognizes the value they have for some people. All he wants to convey is the supremacy of bhakti for the ordinary person who embarks on a spiritual quest while living within the boundaries of the home and the world.

When Chaitanya and his companions reach the point from which the tall spire of the Jagannath temple with its fluttering pennants is visible, he cannot contain himself any longer. Delirious with joy, he leaves the others behind and runs towards the temple. His friends soon catch up, but alas, they are not permitted entry. Everything about them proclaims they are outsiders and after the numerous episodes of hostile incursions the priests are hyper-anxious. They are determined to prevent the agents of the sultan of Bengal from entering the temple with perfidious intentions. Chaitanya is crushed with disappointment, but not for long. Some of his companions like Mukunda Datta follow up on Advaita Acharya's advice and make contact with Gopinath Acharya, brother-in-law to the eminent scholar Sarbabhouma Bhattacharya. Gopinath Acharya goes to the temple to explain who these pilgrims are. Mollified, the priests let them in and at last Chaitanya stands face-to-face with one of the most renowned representations of his beloved lord. He almost swoons with happiness as his dream is fulfilled.

Meeting Sarbabhouma Bhattacharya is also a gratifying event. He is not only a renowned logician and Vedic scholar, but also held in high esteem in royal circles. Members of the city's elite come to him for advice. A native of Nabadwip, Sarbabhouma also knows Chaitanya's family well. He and Chaitanya's late father, Jagannath Misra, were friends and had a relationship of great mutual respect. Although he moved to Puri before Chaitanya's birth, Sarbabhouma has kept up with news from Nabadwip and now is only too eager to help the son of his late friend. Like so many before him, this venerable scholar is also charmed by Chaitanya's sincerity, his sweetness of manner and his intense devotion for Krishna. Above all, he is absolutely struck by the young monk's extraordinary good looks, which have made some describe him as a golden mountain clad in saffron. His long arms, broad chest, elongated, lotus-shaped eyes, his leonine stance, his deep, resounding voice, his firm steps, his bright and joyful face – all add up to convey an impression that no one can forget.

Afterwards, he and his followers discuss the best options for living in Puri. Chaitanya, a true sanyasi who has no regard for material comfort, suggests they build mud huts along the beach and stay there. When he hears this, Sarbabhouma is appalled. He immediately makes arrangements for the group to stay in a house belonging to one of his affluent relatives. Relieved of their housing worries, Chaitanya and his followers are now free to pursue their true objective – worshipping Krishna, chanting his name and immersing themselves in the richly celebratory life of a devotee in Puri. A daily routine of communal devotion and spiritual pursuit falls into place. Occasionally, an all too human levity breaks out in the middle of devotional euphoria as the men engage in playful combat, artfully fighting with sticks as the rural denizens of Brindaban are reputed to have done in Krishna's time. Rolls of laughter fill the halls and perhaps, inside the sacred interior chamber of his temple, Jagannath also smiles.

The weeks fly and gradually the tropical winter

gives way to the fragrant southerly breezes of spring. Soon it will be time for the annual Holi festival – which is a significant part of the lore of Krishna and Radha's time in Brindaban – and Chaitanya joyfully anticipates watching the celebration in Puri. Every morning he goes to the temple, often carrying offerings of milk, yogurt, tulsi leaves and sweets that have been donated to him by prosperous admirers. On most afternoons, one or another of the members of Puri's Vaishnav community invites him and his friends to share a meal, and he accepts with heartfelt appreciation. Sometimes, his friends become the butt of friendly banter about their immense capacity for food. In return, Chaitanya jokes that from now on he and his friends will give up most foods and subsist solely on sweets . . . until, of course, it is time for the next meal.

At last it is time for some of his companions to go back to Nabadwip and resume their regular life. The sweet sorrow of parting is leavened with a sacred sense of mission. Chaitanya urges Nityananda to preach his message all over Bengal with the help of other followers, a task Nityananda will undertake with single-minded passion. He fondly embraces Sribas, whose house in Nabadwip had been the venue of so many kirtan sessions and theatrical performances, and charges him to visit his mother and give her the gifts he is sending from Puri. Whenever he thinks of the sorrow he has caused her by renouncing domestic life, his heart fills with anguish, but he hopes to travel to Nabadwip at some future date and see her again. For each one of his other followers, Raghab, Shibananda, Basudeb and Ramdas, he has a particular injunction and they assure him they will do their best.

The day of departure comes. His friends take leave with great sadness, and till the last moment Chaitanya consoles them and tries to lift their spirits. However, once they have gone, he himself is overcome with sorrow. The experience of jointly undertaking the long and hard journey from Shantipur, the joyful weeks spent in Puri, the communality of being part of a burgeoning, expanding movement – all have forged a bond of fraternal love and friendship that they had not experienced before. Now, left with a small group of friends – Gadadhar, Swarup, Damodar and Gobinda – Chaitanya fashions a routine of spiritual activities that he adheres to with discipline. He meditates, chants, sings, goes to the temple to watch the priests perform the daily rituals of worship in front of Jagannath, and he preaches his message to the visitors who come to meet him. More and more he feels that, although leaving home has been hard, the decision to settle in Puri is the right one. He is full of hope that pilgrims who come from distant parts of India will also take back his message to their home communities. All the time, though, his inner self is intensely seeking a personal, loving bond with Krishna.

~

By the beginning of summer, however, a peculiar restlessness bedevils Chaitanya. Even the proximity of the great Jagannath temple, the opportunity to make daily visits there and pray to his adored god, to sing and chant and dance freely and the freedom from the animosity of Nabadwip's elite Brahmin society are not enough to cure it. He tells his friends he wants to set out travelling again, going southward from Orissa, hoping to reach the Deccan, perhaps even the southernmost point of India where he can see the ancient bridge that Rama built across the ocean to reach the island of Lanka and rescue his wife Sita, who had been abducted by the demon Ravana. This bridge is another marker of Krishna's presence on this earth, for who is Rama but Krishna under another name?

The journey can be both a discovery and a challenge. Chaitanya, like many of his contemporaries, has heard that Hinduism in the south has taken a different shape from that of Bengal or northern India. Religious reformers in the southern provinces have been working hard to minimize the influence of Buddhism and Jainism, which they consider antithetical to the social and spiritual heritage of Hinduism. But unlike in Bengal, where the reformist impetus has found expression in a revitalized expression of Vaishnavism anchored on the devotion to Krishna, the southern reformers have focused on reviving Shaivism as the path of salvation. Chaitanya wonders what kind of encounters he will have with such religious leaders and academics in the south and whether it will bear fruit if he engages in debate with them. Whatever the result, it is a challenge that inspires him.

There is also the personal element. Many of his acquaintances believe that Chaitanya's brother Biswarup had also travelled to southern locations for his own spiritual explorations. It is only natural that he should follow in the footsteps of the beloved, long-lost brother, just in case he can learn more about him.

# 7

# Temple to Road

On a hot summer's day in April, Chaitanya sets out with a few companions. As the bustle of streets, markets and pedestrians of Puri dies down, and the outskirts of the town draw closer, he looks back. The Jagannath temple stands tall, a symbol of immutable divinity, a sanctuary for all who love Krishna. The pennants on its spire respond to the ocean breeze and flutter gracefully, pointing, as always, westward. He had come here with intense expectation, yet he is leaving after four short months. He has not been able to tell his followers exactly why he is so eager to leave a place that had been part of his dreams for so long. He is not even sure he can tell himself – except that there are also other places from where Krishna beckons to him in his dreams.

The cadence of the journey, however, has its own rewards. The group stops in towns, villages and settlements along the way. Chaitanya is a sanyasi who owns nothing and depends on the donation of food for his survival. His companions, necessarily, follow suit. It matters little that they are all from Bengal. Whether in Orissa or anywhere else in India, a monk is always honoured with alms. Sometimes they walk through deserted stretches, and their food supply dwindles. On some days their single meal is sparse indeed, consisting of nothing more than a handful of rice and some sautéed vegetables like bitter gourds. If they are lucky enough to still have some ghee left over from earlier donations, they can pour it over the rice to add extra flavour. Yet, the fellowship of the road and the harmonious communality of their faith make such a meal as good as a sumptuous banquet. The food-loving monk, who was feted with a multi-course meal in the home of Advaita Acharya, the beloved son of a mother who gloried in making his favourite dishes, feels no discontent at sitting down to a minimal repast. He knows that soon enough they will come into more habitable areas and they will again receive the generous donations of people they encounter. Meanwhile, progressing, pausing, resting and meditating about Krishna fill the hours. As he and his followers walk through deeply forested areas, they sometimes lose sight of each other, because of the density of arboreal growth. But the followers have no fear. They know that sooner or later the tall, striking figure of their master will appear between the tree trunks like a beacon to guide them forward. Sometimes the group comes across a pond or a lake and they cast off their clothes and jump into the cool waters, splashing each other, swimming vigorously and roaring with laughter, playful as frolicsome children.

More important, as they make their way through the province, each person Chaitanya meets and talks to provides him with the opportunity to communicate his message about focusing on bhakti as the simplest yet best path to find Krishna. For those who are far from the temple of Jagannath and do not have the ability to get there, for those who are despised by the upper echelons of society, for those who lack the resources to hire priests and perform ritual, the chanting of the Hare Krishna mantra is all that is needed to bring Jagannath to them, says Chaitanya.

Approaching the Godavari river near the southern border of Orissa, Chaitanya sends word through the local residents that he would like to meet Ramananda Ray, the viceroy of Orissa's Rajmahendri province and one of the most powerful and trusted representatives of King Prataparudra. When Chaitanya first announced his plans for travelling south, Sarbabhouma Bhattacharya had advised him to contact Ray, who is not only a devout Vaishnav, but also a poet and dramatist. Ray and his brothers all hold high positions in the administration of the king and, in these times of frequent military conflict and ensuing upheavals, Sarbabhouma wisely judged that a powerful official would be a helpful person for Chaitanya to contact. What he may not have anticipated is the electrifying impact that the young monk would have on this powerful royal viceroy.

Ramananda Ray welcomes Chaitanya with utmost hospitality and graciousness, inviting him to stay in Rajmahendri as long as he desires. Chaitanya, too, is happy to take a break. They spend long hours in conversation, quoting their favourite passages from poetry and debating profound philosophical questions. When it is time to leave, Chaitanya repeatedly asks Ramananda Ray to visit him in Puri when he is back there. As they say farewell, the two feel bonded with the strongest possible attachment between a master and his disciple. Ray promises Chaitanya he will meet him in Puri at some future date.

By the time Chaitanya and his followers reach Setubandha, the ancient bridge built by Rama to cross the ocean channel and reach the island of Lanka, they are both replete and exhausted. Chaitanya's encounters with scholars and priests at academic centres and temples have been rich with stimulating discourse. Many southern Vaishnavs have remained sceptical about his primary message – that chanting the Hare Krishna mantra is as effective a means to reach god as any orthodox ritual or prayer – yet they have also been astonished and impressed by his eloquence, his fervour, his humility and his tolerance for all men. They will surely never forget him. For his part, he is carrying precious mementos of this southern sojourn – two holy texts, the *Brahmasamhita*, consisting of verses spoken by the god Brahma as a prayer to Krishna, and the *Srikrishnakarnamrita*, a rapturous eulogy of Krishna's greatness composed by the southern poet Bilwamangal. Chaitanya has had both books copied. In the coming years, he will read the verses and recite them to his followers, as a means to comprehend the supreme glory of Krishna.

Now, however, both Chaitanya and his band of followers are more than ready to make their way back to Puri. It will be another long and difficult trek, but the vision of the Jagannath temple remains a steady beacon before their eyes and draws them back. By the time they reach Puri, it is May 1512. They have been gone for more than two years. They know Sarbabhouma Bhattacharya will welcome them with enthusiasm. More important, they will once again enter the temple, look on the image of Jagannath, pray to him and chant his many names. Throughout the return journey, Chaitanya moves with the eagerness of a lover who has been parted from his beloved all too long.

Alas, another disappointment awaits him, worse than the let-down he experienced when he first came to Puri from Shantipur. It is a matter of timing, not of conflict and chaos. He has arrived just at the beginning of the Snanjatra festival when all three images – Jagannath and his two siblings – are taken outside the temple and given a ritual bath. A well-known legend pertaining to the festival has a long life. Apparently, Jagannath and his siblings fell ill with fever after the bath and it took them two weeks to recover. The priests, in a re-enactment of this ancient story, keep the images in seclusion for that period during which no one is allowed to see them.

For Chaitanya, in whose mind god has become more and more of an intimate presence, it is a severe blow. He finds himself unable to bear the weight of crushing disappointment. Two weeks is not a long time, yet he reacts like an impatient lover who cannot bear the torture of not being able to see his beloved even when distance is not an issue. With an impetuosity that brooks no objection from friends and followers, he decides to leave Puri again and go back to spend some time in southern Orissa. When Ramananda Ray hears of this, he arranges to meet Chaitanya by the Godavari river. Once again, it is a meeting of delighted minds. Instead of going back to his home, Ray ends up staying with Chaitanya, whom he now considers as good as his guru, for four months.

~

It is October before Chaitanya returns to Puri, again carrying Ramananda Ray's assurance that at some future date they will meet in Puri. Because of his impulsive turnaround, because he could not wait two weeks, he has missed the great annual festival of the Jagannath temple – Rathajatra. But the enigmatic part of his personality makes it impossible for anyone to decipher whether he regrets his decision. When it is time for the festival the following year, he not only has the opportunity to participate, he also has the company of old friends and followers from Bengal who have come to see him: the venerable Advaita Acharya, Chaitanya's old schoolmate Murari Gupta, Haridas, the elderly Muslim convert whom he so loves, Sribas, who used to generously throw open his house for the Vaishnavs of Nabadwip to gather and sing kirtans, Raghab Pandit and several others, as well as two hundred Vaishnav pilgrims from different parts of Bengal.

It is an amazing, lively gathering. For the first time, Chaitanya and the visitors from Bengal join the huge throngs that accompany the chariots as they progress down the main road from the Jagannath temple to the Gundicha temple. Along the way, the group of followers surrounds Chaitanya to protect him from the crowd and they all raise their voices in singing kirtans honouring Krishna. Chaitanya is beside himself. Consumed with mystic rapture, he sometimes raises his voice so that it becomes a roar; he dances with frenzy, arms upraised, eyes closed, not caring where he steps; slowing down, he treads heavily, his head and body swaying from side to side like an impatient elephant's. He looks about him as if he wonders how to break free from the press of people around him, and the next moment, tapping a source of some superhuman energy, he whirls round and round like a man on fire. The crowd has never seen someone like this and they are both awed and entranced. For most of them, it will be a vision permanently etched in their memories.

The celebration of Rathajatra this year is doubly memorable for the Vaishnav visitors from Nabadwip, Shantipur and other places in

Bengal because it is on this occasion that Advaita Acharya publicly declares his long-held belief that Chaitanya is none other than an incarnation of Krishna. He arranges a special session of kirtan that honours both Chaitanya and Krishna as two parts of the same whole. The friends and followers rejoice and look forward to the future when they will share this truth with others in Bengal. When the festival concludes, the visitors stay on in Puri, spending almost four months with Chaitanya. As always, when the time for parting comes, it is grievously sorrowful. By way of consolation, Chaitanya asks them to make plans to visit him every year during Rathajatra. It is not a realistic prospect, since travel between Bengal and Orissa still remains hazardous, both because of road conditions and because of the uncertainties of ongoing cross-border conflict. Besides, for most people, it is not practicable to set aside the funds for such a journey every year and abandon their livelihood for the couple of months that such a trip would entail. Still it is a comforting possibility to keep in mind and it underlines the tender affection and concern that their master feels for them.

One day Sarbabhouma Bhattacharya comes to

visit Chaitanya. The temporary accommodation that the former had arranged for Chaitanya when he first came to Puri is no longer needed. Instead, Chaitanya and his intimate friends are being housed in a small country home belonging to Kashi Misra, one of the senior managers of the Jagannath temple. After two years of travels in the south, Sarbabhouma Bhattacharya thinks Chaitanya deserves to enjoy some rest and physical comfort and be feted with a special meal. Humbly, he requests the young monk to be his guest and live in his house for a month. Chaitanya, however, cannot accept. It is impossible for a man whose vows entail renunciation to return to the comforts of domestic life. But Sarbabhouma is unwilling to give up so easily. After much pleading, Chaitanya agrees to come and stay with him for five days. The generous old man, aware of Chaitanya's attachment to his remaining friends, suggests that they should come to his house every day at mealtimes, a prospect that delights Chaitanya.

When Sarbabhouma's wife hears about Chaitanya being their guest, she is overjoyed. Like Shachi and Advaita Acharya's wife, she is a cook of great repute and, like her husband, she too is very taken with this lovable, unworldly young man from Nabadwip. She gets to work, preparing her best dishes. When the first meal is served, Chaitanya and his friends are amazed. It is a feast that is reminiscent of the one served at Advaita Acharya's home in Shantipur. For a monk and his followers, used to a meagre diet of rice and vegetables, occasionally supplemented with milk or yogurt, this is indeed a kingly repast. As in Advaita Acharya's house, the meal is served on a whole banana leaf, the centrepiece being a mound of fine white rice. Fragrant ghee, poured over it, moistens the rice and runs in little rivulets on to the surface of the leaf. Small containers, made with the leaves of the fragrant keya plant so prolific in Orissa, are arranged around the banana leaf. There are many kinds of greens; some vegetables prepared with the bitter leaves of neem, others seasoned with black pepper; fried pellets of ground dal; pumpkin and white gourd cooked with milk; banana blossom prepared in two different ways; a savoury dish that is also seasoned with sugar; slices of fried vegetables like aubergine, pumpkin and taro; two kinds of soupy dal; five or six kinds of tart preparations; and of course, a large variety of sweets made with coconut, ground dal and evaporated milk. As if this is not enough, there are bowls of yogurt and platters of fruits like bananas and mangos, some of them blended with thickened milk. It is little short of a miracle for a woman to have produced such a feast in the confines of a home kitchen and in the space of a few hours. Chaitanya praises his hostess and expresses deep appreciation for her cooking, but she and her husband modestly disclaim all credit. It is Krishna who has prepared everything, they say, pointing to the leaves of the tulsi, the holy basil plant, that sit on the cover of each serving platter. In the mind of a Vaishnav, tulsi is almost synonymous with Krishna.

# 8

# The Travelling Monk

The restlessness that propelled Chaitanya southward has not subsided. After a few months in Puri, he starts talking about making another long journey, this time north to Mathura and Brindaban. All his friends advise him to wait until conditions improve. After all, the trip would entail going through Bengal, where the sultan's army is still engaged in sporadic raids and battles along the border with Orissa. Chaitanya is impatient, but eventually he accedes to their request. One of the benefits of delaying the journey is the opportunity to spend time with Ramananda Ray, who has left his province and his palace to come to Puri with his whole family. Chaitanya has become, for the time being, the centre of their world and he, in turn, enjoys engaging in spiritual discourse, communal chanting and singing of kirtan with them.

By the autumn of 1514, the conflict winds down and the resulting peaceful conditions make travel safe again. Chaitanya decides to travel first to Bengal – to the capital Gaur, and then to his birthplace Nabadwip and on to Shantipur, where Advaita Acharya lives. After that, he will make his way to Mathura and Brindaban, two holy sites he had wanted to visit earlier, but was dissuaded by Nityananda and others. Anticipating another long separation, Sarbabhouma Bhattacharya and Ramananda Ray both join Chaitanya's group of friends as they set out north from Puri. Sarbabhouma says farewell to the travellers in Cuttack and Ramananda accompanies them all the way to Bhadrak before returning to Puri.

Although the prospect of being embroiled in combat is no longer there, travel has its other hazards. Their route takes them through long stretches of rough terrain and across rivers until they reach Panihati in Bengal. From there, they decide to travel by road along the banks of the Ganga until they will reach Gaur and then Nabadwip. But word travels fast and the return of

Chaitanya to his homeland is an exciting event. When he left Nabadwip, he was known to a small but growing coterie of Vaishnavs as a stimulating leader. Now, partly because of the work done by followers like Nityananda, his fame has spread far and wide. From towns and villages, people come in droves in the hope of setting eyes on this saintly figure and obtaining his blessings. By the time he reaches Ramkeli, it is summer of 1515, and the crowds following him are bigger than ever. This tiny village will remember Chaitanya's arrival for centuries, commemorating him with an annual religious fair.

It is not just the public in Bengal that is astir. Sultan Hussain Shah's ministers have also heard about a young monk who is making his way towards the capital city, Gaur, with an enormous entourage. Wondering what impact his arrival might have, they instruct their local officials and guards to keep an eye on Chaitanya and prevent any unruly activity. But even in the sultan's court, there are people who are neither surprised at his ability to draw people nor unaware of his role as a leader and reformer of the Vaishnav community. Two of them are brothers working for the sultan.

He has given them positions of responsibility and the honourable titles of Dabir-i-Khas and Sakar Mallik. For some time now they have been secretly writing letters to Chaitanya in Puri, expressing their intense desire to become his disciples and immerse themselves in the practice of Vaishnavism according to his teachings. On hearing of his arrival in Ramkeli, they leave the court in disguise and come to meet him face-to-face. True to his nature, Chaitanya embraces them with unquestioning love and accepts them as disciples. He also asks them to discard the identities they have acquired in the sultan's court. Sakar Mallik, he says, will be known as Rupa and Dabir-i-Khas as Sanatan. The brothers discuss Chaitanya's travel plans and advise him to abandon his idea of going all the way to Mathura and Brindaban until things settle down some more. For now, they tell him, it is better to leave quietly, before the crowds of followers are aware of his departure.

Unlike the many times when Chaitanya has stubbornly refused to change his plans, he takes their advice. Before leaving, he asks the brothers to join him later, when he finally does get to Brindaban. Does he also know what the future has in store for Sanatan? For the sultan will find out that his trusted official wants to leave his job to join a monk as his disciple. Angry at what seems stark ingratitude, Hussain Shah will keep him under house arrest for an indefinite period. It is only by luck and careful planning that Sanatan will eventually manage to disguise himself and escape, joining his brother to meet Chaitanya. Some years later, the two brothers will commit themselves to fulfil their master's desire to make Brindaban – Krishna's legendary birthplace, home to Vaishnav believers for many years – come to life again as a prime centre of Vaishnav spirituality. But before they can make much progress, poor Sanatan will again be assailed by misfortune. Afflicted by a strange and apparently incurable disease, he will be too disheartened to continue his spiritual and proselytizing tasks. Instead, he will make his way to Puri. Chaitanya will again embrace him warmly, find him a place to stay and do his utmost to restore his spirits until he can go back to Brindaban.

~

That, however, is in the future. For now, it is time for Chaitanya to take leave of these two brothers and go homeward to spend time in familiar territory, see his old friends and perhaps even his beloved mother. His arrival in Shantipur is greeted with rapturous joy by all his friends and followers. As before, he comes to stay in Advaita Acharya's house and members of the Vaishnav community pour in to see him, talk to him, touch him, chant with him and sing and dance with him. The sound of the Hare Krishna mantra rises in the air, accompanied by the combined music of drums, cymbals and bells. Many members of the community invite him to visit and he obliges, moving from home to home, village to village. Days flow into weeks; weeks flow into months.

When, finally, he comes back to Advaita Acharya's house, his host recommends that a message be sent to Shachi, apprising her of her son's return to Shantipur. Acharya wants to invite her to his house. Whether or not he is aware of her one-time reservations about him, no one knows better than he how heartbroken Shachi is at the loss of her last remaining child. Having been a friend of the family for long, he is all too aware of the tragic losses she has suffered in childbirth, as well as the shock she and her husband experienced when their older son, Biswarup, left home to become a monk. Biswarup has vanished; rumours say he is dead. But Chaitanya, Shachi's darling Nimai, is here, even though he can never go home to her. Advaita Acharya wants to make sure that she gets to see him before he again sets off on his travels. A few days together in Shantipur will be a precious memory for both of them and sustain Shachi during the long, mournful years to come.

When Shachi arrives at his house, Advaita and his wife greet her respectfully and ask if she will prepare a meal for her son who is unlikely to have too many opportunities of eating well or relishing the particular delicacies she excels at once he starts on the road to Mathura and Brindaban. Can a mother say anything but yes? Shachi is only too delighted to have this opportunity.

Coming face-to-face with her son, whom she has not seen since he left home to take his vows of renunciation, fills her with both joy and anguish. Yes, she had expected to see a radical transformation. Still it is a shock. Her handsome son, her mischievous Nimai, stands before her as

Chaitanya the monk, his head shaven, dressed in a saffron dhoti and little else, his face and body marked by hardship, a picture of austerity and sacrifice. Overcome with emotion, mother and son hold each other and mingle their tears. Shachi remembers the long-gone night of the eclipse when her son's appearance had lit up her world and she had held him close to her heart and listened to his breath. Now she fears she will never see him again.

As a mother, however, it is her duty to put away her sorrow, wipe her tears and do what she wants to do more than anything else – prepare a memorable meal that will include her son's particular favourites. When the meal is served, Advaita's household as well as Chaitanya's friends gathers around to watch him eat his mother's dishes. He samples every item with delight, but what he most enjoys on this occasion are the different greens that Shachi has prepared, each in a distinctive way. Seeing how he helps himself repeatedly, his friends and followers smile fondly. Chaitanya is not in the least embarrassed. Rather, he reminds them that food is not mere bodily sustenance, it has spiritual connotations that too often we fail to remember. The only food that we should eat is what is also fit to be offered to Krishna. To illustrate the goodness of greens, he points to a variety called achyuta and says that consuming it arouses deep devotion for Krishna. The bitter leaves of patol and some other vegetables confer the blessing of always being in the company of true Vaishnavs. As for other varieties like salancha and helancha, they keep the body free from all ailments, thus helping us to concentrate wholeheartedly on worshipping Krishna.

~

Travels in Bengal concluded, Chaitanya returns to Puri for a short hiatus before starting on the road to Mathura and Brindaban. As before, he is accompanied by a few faithful followers. This time they have to make their way through the northern and western stretches of Bengal, known as Jharikhand – an area of extensive forests and wilderness stretching from Katwa to Birbhum – until they reach populous areas. Their first significant halt, however, is not Brindaban, but another holy city – Kashi, also called Varanasi. Here, after many years, Chaitanya meets Tapan Misra, whom he had encountered when, after his marriage to Lakshmi, he had travelled to his home village in the eastern Bengali district of Sylhet. Tapan Misra's son, Raghunath, is now an adult and, like so many other devout Vaishnavs, he, too, wants to become a disciple of Chaitanya. In later years, he will be known as Raghunath Bhatta, and he will join forces with the brothers Rupa and Sanatan in Brindaban.

At last, the ultimate goal of the Vaishnav traveller is at hand. Chaitanya, reaching Mathura and Brindaban, visits all the legendary sites associated with the activities of Krishna as a child and a young man among the community of cowherds. Before his eyes, the mythical past becomes the immediate present. He sees his beloved Krishna, playful and mischievous as a boy, passionate and tender as Radha's lover, performing unexpected miracles for the rural inhabitants of Brindaban and frolicking joyfully with the milkmaids who shower him with undiluted love. Overwhelmed by such visions, Chaitanya relapses into a series of fits and trances and bouts of ecstatic frenzy that were first seen in Nabadwip when he was a young man. Outsiders who see him are amazed at these manifestations. But there is also something about him that generates a response of awe and devotion even among strangers. This, they feel, is no ordinary madman. Whatever ails him is akin to a divine madness. Still, his companions decide it is not safe to stay in a place that arouses such extreme reactions in him. Despite his protests, they leave the area and travel to Prayag (Allahabad), a place made sacred by the confluence of the holy rivers Ganga and Jamuna and the subterranean Saraswati.

In Prayag, Chaitanya seems to recover some degree of normalcy, but episodically lapses into abnormal behaviour. Once, escaping from his watchful companions, he wanders away by himself. As in Brindaban and Mathura, he is again overcome by a vivid vision of a group of cowherds playing the flute and falls into a swoon. Several Muslim riders, who happened to be passing by, dismount to see if he is dead. From the marks of tears on his face and froth around his mouth, they conclude he has been poisoned, until he suddenly opens his eyes, sits up and says in a most rational manner, 'I just had an epileptic fit.' His frantic companions come up at this juncture, and are only too relieved to find him safe and unhurt.

In Prayag, there is a delightful encounter when Rupa, who has been waiting for word of his arrival, comes to meet him. As he and Sanatan had said earlier, they are determined to forsake the worldly life and join Chaitanya. Rupa has managed to dispose of all his property and assets before leaving Bengal, but Sanatan is still under arrest. Still, Rupa is confident that his brother will soon find a way out of prison and meet with them. After spending a few days together, Chaitanya instructs Rupa to travel to Puri, where he will join him later. His own goal now is revisiting Kashi, where Tapan Misra is waiting and where he plans to stay a couple of months, immersing himself in the life of the holy city of light. And as if Krishna himself has taken charge of events, Sanatan unexpectedly arrives in Kashi to join Chaitanya. He has escaped by bribing the prison guards and now is free to devote himself in lifelong service of Chaitanya and his mission.

~

When Chaitanya finally returns to Puri, several of his followers from Bengal come to visit him and give him news of Nabadwip. Ramananda Ray is also there, as is Paramananda Puri, a much older monk who had been acquainted with Biswarup. Chaitanya settles down in the house and compound that the Puri temple administrator had set aside for him. A coterie of the faithful joins him. Among them are his childhood friend Gadadhar, Swarup Damodar, Jagadananda, Raghunath Das, Haridas, Damodar Pandit, to name a few. Each tries to take on a specific role to help the master. Gadadhar is the faithful shadow. Swarup, because of his deep knowledge and appreciation of literature, reads aloud from Chaitanya's favourite poetic texts. If a new text is brought forward, it is Swarup's responsibility to make sure there is nothing in it that will disturb Chaitanya's refined tastes. Haridas is too old to do much, but his mere presence is a source of pleasure for Chaitanya who makes sure that the old man is well looked after. Haridas has never forgotten his Muslim origins and has always considered himself unworthy to step inside the Jagannath temple as all the others do. From his little cottage he looks up at the temple spire with its fluttering pennants and offers his prayers. Chaitanya finds such humility exemplary in a Vaishnav and his love for the old man has deepened because of it. Jagadananda, who is also from Nabadwip, has taken charge of the master's diet and sometimes he has arguments with the others about what is suitable and what is not. Chaitanya enjoins him to visit Nabadwip twice a year to get news of Shachi.

A simple routine falls into place. Neither Chaitanya nor any of his followers knows if he will suddenly declare the intention of travelling again. Until he does so, the followers are only too happy to tend to him and make sure he is well and happy. He starts his day with a visit to the Jagannath temple. Back at the estate, he spends several hours loudly chanting the Hare Krishna mantra. He does not go out like other monks to beg for food donations. Instead, he has lunch at the house of any one of his many devotees in Puri who do not mind feeding his closest followers too. As he did during his tutoring days in Nabadwip, he takes a nap after lunch. When he wakes, one of his followers, Gobinda, who had once worked for Sarbabhouma Bhattacharya, massages his legs and feet. Later in the afternoon and evening, he meets with visitors, some of whom come from far away.

Many of Chaitanya's Nabadwip associates, such as Advaita Acharya, come to see him from time to time. They bring news from home, not all of it always welcome. Some of them have been riled by Nityananda's arrogant manner as he goes around spreading Chaitanya's message to the people of Bengal. Having discarded all belief in caste and ritual, Nityananda has no problem occasionally staying in the homes of people belonging to the lowest rungs of the caste ladder and eating and drinking with them. Chaitanya, however, brushes aside such complaints, since he himself has done the same at one time or another. He even reveals to some of his close disciples that it was the small-mindedness and criticism directed at him by some of Nabadwip's elite which had prompted him to take his renunciation vows and leave the town for good.

A more welcome diversion comes when visitors from home come bearing gifts. The sister of one of Chaitanya's followers takes every opportunity to send jars of kasundi or Bengali mustard, often flavoured with mango or ginger, home-made sweets, pickles made with different fruits and spices, fine-quality parched rice and puffed rice. These are offerings of devoted love and Chaitanya accepts them with childlike delight. Often he requests Jagadananda to serve the pickles and mustard during meals.

It is, on the whole, a joyful time for this little group. Even the episodes of trances and swoons seem to have reduced. Chaitanya can fully engage in the life he has chosen and rejoice at the thought that travelling pilgrims from all over India may be taking his message back with them to their respective home towns.

# 9

# Master and Disciples

In a shaded garden near a small shrine in Puri, Chaitanya sits surrounded by his disciples and friends. The monsoon is over and the great chariot festival has been celebrated with euphoric splendour. Now, with the departure of the crowds, it is a quiet time, a lull between the seasons when the monsoon is withdrawing and autumn is touching the world with tentative fingers. The tall spire of the Jagannath temple, with its pennant fluttering in the wind, is visible from where the group is assembled. From time to time, Chaitanya's eyes turn that way and he stops speaking as if his train of thought had fallen away and a potent force is taking over his whole consciousness. But he does not fall into a trance, nor does he burst into tears. No, today is different. Today, he is able to refocus on the faces that are looking at him with intense adoration and he can resume his discourse on what matters to him most – the nature of bhakti, the qualities that make a true Vaishnav, the intensity of joy that comes to the devotee who forgets the self through chanting and singing and feels the nearness of Krishna, the blue-skinned god. The people sitting with him have come from different parts of Bengal and Orissa, as well as from other towns in India like Kashi and Brindaban. Some are high-caste, scholarly men, some are ordinary folk who make a living by commerce or agriculture, some are young and ardent, some elderly and marked by the vicissitudes of life. Among them are the special ones who are gearing up to ensure that Chaitanya's message will live forever and transform the way people think of god. They look like they cannot have enough of the master's words and thoughts as they listen with the utmost intentness, striving to find many dimensions of meaning in the simple words that he speaks.

He is not saying anything fundamentally new. Many of the listeners have heard him say the same thing, yet each time he manages to find a different way to bring his ideas to them. A master of metaphor, he draws parallels from ancient scripture and medieval poetry to expound the profundity behind apparently simple concepts. As always, his primary theme is bhakti, the heartfelt devotion that can enable a person – rich or poor, learned or ignorant, ascetic or householder – to reach Krishna. Among the younger acolytes, some wonder why bhakti should be superior to other ways of worship, why it is better than jnana (knowledge) or karma (action) or yoga (meditation). Chaitanya answers like the humanist he proved himself to be in his early days as a Vaishnav in Nabadwip. Bhakti, he points out, is universally accessible. Any person can summon up loving devotion for god from the depths of his heart, regardless of his or her social status, wealth, education or physical ability. To pursue god through knowledge or meditation can only be possible for those who have had the privilege of education and training, just as action is the preserve of those who have power, who are not the downtrodden or the outcastes.

A young listener asks whether renouncing the world is a superior path to god than being an ordinary householder, since a sanyasi, free from worldly distractions and ties, can devote all his energies, his entire wealth of bhakti, to the quest. Chaitanya rejects that supposition with utter conviction. He himself has become a sanyasi because he was drawn to that path and also because he had come to believe that rejecting domestic life in Nabadwip would enable him to reach the largest number of people. But he has never forgotten the heavy price that had to be paid for renunciation. His mother's desolation, his wife's mute grief – neither is likely to be forgotten or dismissed. Although some might choose that same rigorous path for reasons of their own, it is important to remember, he points out, that reaching Krishna through devotional love does not depend on whether you live in the world or reject it. The exquisiteness of bhakti lies in its rootedness in five kinds of love that merge to form a five-petalled flower – shanta (peaceful), dasya (submissive), sakhya (friendly), batsalya (filial) and madhur (sweet). He himself learned this many years ago from that great Vaishnav devotee Ramananda Ray, and every day brings home to him the truth of this idea. A Vaishnav's love for Krishna is not an emotion isolated from all other feelings; it draws on his or her relationship with parents, siblings, spouse, children and friends. Thus the love we feel for human beings becomes the stepping stone to our deepest love for god and finds its full expression in these five ways. That is why being a devoted Vaishnav is just as possible for a householder as it is for a sanyasi. Had he lived in another age, Chaitanya might have phrased it differently, describing the Vaishnav way of life as the most democratic path to the divine. But as he speaks to the young acolytes, he notes with pleasure that his words are sinking into their minds and flowering into realizations.

When most of the listeners are gone, a small group still stays with him, long-time associates like Swarup, Damodar, Raghunath, Gadadhar and Rupa. They are his nearest and dearest and the love he extends to them is only second to the love he feels for Krishna. Perhaps the most brilliant one of the group is Rupa, and today he is more than usually intent on assimilating his guru's profoundest thoughts. How are we to identify a true Vaishnav, he wonders, and the others echo the question. This is something they have been thinking about for a long time. Chaitanya smiles, as if the answer is all too obvious. 'A true Vaishnav always has the name of Krishna on his lips,' he says. Surely it cannot be that simple? Chaitanya sees the seeds of confusion in their eyes and provides a further definition: 'If the mere sight of a person brings the name of Krishna to the lips of all who meet him or her, you can be sure that person is the best of Vaishnavs.' This strikes home, for indeed the disciples are seeing the best of all Vaishnavs in the figure of Chaitanya. As master and disciples look at each other with joyful love, Krishna's name rises to everyone's lips. In an unusually discursive mood, Chaitanya continues to define the essence of Vaishnavism: 'Be lower than the smallest blade of grass, be as patient as a tree, treat even the humblest person with respect, and always chant the name of the lord.'

Suddenly, his eyes close, his palms join together and an emotive intensity fills his face and voice. From instructions for followers, his words change to become a prayer:

> Lord, I don't desire wealth or power or beautiful women. All I want is that throughout the cycle of rebirth, my devotion to you should remain steadfast. Let the name of Krishna be forever

triumphant, for it purifies our minds, quenches the fires of worldly life, bestows goodness and joy, gives us the taste of eternal peace and is the source of all knowledge. Lord, although there is no prescribed hour of day when I should recite all your names in order to acquire fortitude to face all my troubles, I still fail to do so. Son of Nanda, I am your servant, and I am floundering in the perilous ocean of this worldly life. Consider me the tiniest grain of dust under your feet. I long for the moment when taking your name will fill my eyes with tears of joy, silence my tongue and make me tremble with love. In your absence, every moment feels like an age. My anguished tears flow unchecked and the whole world seems empty. Whether he crushes me in his embrace or grieves me by not letting me see him, it is Krishna who is the lord of my heart.

The words swirl around them on the westerly ocean breeze and each one of the disciples is moved as never before. Rupa, who more than any of the other disciples, is entrusted with the mission of spreading his guru's message, immediately records these words. Later, he will title them the

*Shikshashtaka* and urge all Vaishnavs to recite them daily as they meditate on the nature of bhakti.

~

Often Chaitanya refers to the works of Vaishnav poets like Vidyapati and Chandidas as well as their predecessor, Joydeb, the composer of the *Gita Gobinda*. All of them have depicted the intensely passionate relationship between Krishna and Radha as well as Krishna's affectionate relationship with Radha's friends and the milkmaids of Brindaban. Collectively, their works are referred to as *Mahajanapada*, the compositions of the great ones. Chaitanya has delved deep into them and can quote at length from verses rich in alliteration, allusion, metaphor and meaning. He also loves listening when a friend like Swarup recites the texts or when someone sings verses put to music.

The enjoyment of poetry, however, is not the sole purpose behind Chaitanya's preoccupation with these works. What seems, on the surface, to be a charming story about the love between a man and a woman in a particular space and time, or the mysterious relationship between divine and mythical figures, is actually, he tells his disciples, a profound illustration of the selfless love, free of expectation, which all Vaishnavs must strive to offer Krishna. Repeatedly, these poets have demonstrated how to refute the concept of possessive, all-exclusive, desire-fuelled love. Krishna in these poems is not an all-powerful deity charged with the preservation of the world, but a charming, lovable young cowherd, brought up as the son of a dairy farmer in Brindaban. He is showered with the love of all who come close to him – parents, playmates and, as he grows older, the young maidens of the community. He has plenty of human foibles. When he and Radha – the wife of a prosperous farmer – fall in love, they act like any pair of illicit lovers. They meet in secret and quench their passion. Radha takes the most extraordinary risks to secretly leave her home in the dead of night and meet him in the wooded areas near the Jamuna river. Even the most erotic of passages in these Vaishnav texts seem inadequate to convey the depth of their passion.

But – and here is the contradiction that Chaitanya loves to dwell on – in his mind, it is not the themes of infidelity or carnal desire that the verses are focusing on. In this particular poetic universe, the love that Radha offers Krishna is so pure and selfless that it negates all associations of sinful conduct. She is the emblem of the soul – a soul that a Vaishnav should aspire to have – which loses itself in Krishna. Her body becomes the offering presented by a devotee to god. No journey to such a divine union can be free of difficulties.

Chaitanya elucidates all the elements of risk, danger and suspense that are inherent in the situation. For a married woman, the only way to meet a lover is to plan a secret tryst, in this case a secluded, wooded area by the river. To get there, especially on a pitch-black rainy night, she has to take great precautions to avoid detection and prepare for the conditions of the journey. So she pours water on the courtyard of her house and practises walking on the slippery surface that mimics the wet paths in the forest. She pricks the soles of her feet with sharp objects to inure herself to the pain of feeling sharp thorns underfoot. She wraps cloths around her ankle bells, to muffle their sound. She puts on a dark sari, the same colour as her lover's skin, to avoid being seen as she makes her way to where he is waiting. What is all this, says Chaitanya, but the preparation of the soul to overcome all obstacles that stand in the way of reaching god? And what of Krishna, the divine lover? He is not merely a careless youth enjoying the pleasure of dalliance. He, too, is waiting, and waiting, and waiting, eager with expectation, to receive the beloved who is taking such risks. Any delay fills him with anxiety. The slightest sound makes him look around eagerly for her. Each time the wind blows through the branches and a leaf drops to the forest floor, he thinks he hears her footsteps. And when she does not appear, he is consumed with agony. It is important to remember, says Chaitanya, that Krishna is not only yearning to receive, he is also intent on giving.

Radha and Krishna are not the sole symbols of the selfless love that Chaitanya urges all his disciples to cultivate. Perhaps surprisingly, he dwells on the role of the gopis, or milkmaids, of Brindaban. Just like Radha, they, too, are deeply in love with Krishna. He is one and they are many. Can that be an obstacle? Again, not if the nature of the love between them consists of overflowing generosity, rather than mere carnality. Since Krishna is aware that the milkmaids are content only to love, he responds in kind, engaging in intimacies and playfulness with them. The gopis know that no one is more cherished than Radha, yet they are not afflicted with anger or jealousy. Sometimes, it is Radha who falls prey to such emotions, especially if Krishna has kept her waiting while he is engaged with the gopis. Like all human beings, she, too, is not perfect. But her love is so true that she can never hold on to her anger or disappointment when he throws himself at her feet and begs forgiveness. This, to the Vaishnav, is yet another example of how important the beloved is to Krishna. Chaitanya urges all his followers to remember that as they try to concentrate on the path of bhakti, even as they are undergoing the struggles and distractions of daily life. And perhaps most unusual of all, he tells them to emulate the gopis, to love Krishna without expectation, jealousy or possessiveness. Should they be able to do so, Krishna will be enshrined forever in their hearts.

While many perceive Chaitanya during his lifetime as an incarnation of Krishna himself, some of his future followers will see him differently. They will ponder on these concepts of selfless love as recorded by his disciples and they will identify Chaitanya with Radha even though she is feminine. To these followers, his description of Radha as the incarnation of true love could only have been based on his identifying with her as he pursued Krishna through the maze of worldly existence. They will remember how Chaitanya loved to quote and listen to the moving passages composed by poets like Vidyapati about biraha – the unendurable pangs of separation suffered by Radha – and they will see him become the personalization of the poets' verses. In some temples, where the images of blue-skinned Krishna and his golden Radha are worshipped together, worshippers will gaze on them and their love for Chaitanya will enclose Radha and make her their beloved lord.

# 10

# Eclipse

One, two, three – the years lengthen into a decade and beyond. For nearly twelve years now, Chaitanya has remained continuously in Puri, engrossed in his meditative quest for Krishna's love. People have come to see him in many different ways – saint, mystic, devotee, a modern incarnation of Krishna, an embodiment of the selfless love that Radha and the gopis of Brindaban offered Krishna, the beloved son of Nabadwip, the most precious gift in his mother's life. Commoners, nobility, scholars and even royalty are mesmerized by his words, his vision and the unquestioning, open-hearted acceptance he offers to those who come to him. They refer to him as Mahaprabhu, the great master. He has become a living legend in a town where people have come for centuries to pray before the images in the temple of Jagannath. Some have even begun to believe that Chaitanya and Jagannath are but two sides of the same divinity.

Chaitanya, however, hardly notices the effect he has on people, the devotion he has aroused in the multitudes and the unexpected change he has effected in the hearts of those who were once most sceptical. For all the years that he has not been travelling, he has been content to spend time either in and around the temple of Jagannath or in the smaller neighbourhood shrines, as if he is perpetually engaged in an inner colloquy with Krishna. At times he asks his followers to read aloud verses from Vaishnav poems or the holy Sanskrit text *Srimadbhagavatam*. At other times, he goes for long, meditative walks along the seashore or stops to visit his faithful elderly follower Haridas, who still lives his life of solitary devotion in a cottage near the temple.

The master who once exhorted his followers to fill the streets and homes with the resounding melody of the holy chant of Hare Krishna, who sat with them and expounded at length on the nature of bhakti as the path to god, no longer expends his energy on evangelizing. Having already entrusted his most trusted disciples in

Brindaban, Bengal and Orissa with the task, he is confident they will carry it out faithfully. Most of the time he is in a state of ecstatic reverie, like a man possessed, striving for union with the god he loves, seeing him here, there, everywhere. For long intervals, he even seems unaware of hunger and thirst. He lies on the ground, weeping with longing or smiling at the thought of union with his sweet lord, indifferent to the dust and grime besmirching his golden skin and saffron clothing. At times, thinking he can hear Krishna calling, he starts running towards an unseen destination until he falls down in exhaustion. When he walks on the pale sands of the beach at Puri, he sometimes imagines he can see the beloved form of Krishna limned in the surging ocean waves which, in his eyes, have become the dark waters of the Jamuna river in Brindaban. Feverish with desire, he throws himself into the water in the hope of losing himself in the divine. He only survives because the watchful friends and disciples who always accompany him are able to pull him out of the sea. On one such occasion, he launches into a vivid description of the erotic play between Krishna and the milkmaids of Brindaban, which he claims to have witnessed when he was submerged in water. There is no doubt that his sense of reality has become starkly disconnected from that of the world around him.

The small band of the faithful who stay close to him make sure that his physical needs are met, that he is safe and protected despite the vulnerability resulting from his euphoric state of mind, that he does not succumb to accident or illness. The one who is almost inseparable from him is the friend of his youth, Gadadhar Misra. Wherever Chaitanya goes, we can see Gadadhar following him. When Chaitanya falls to the ground, it is Gadadhar who is the first to raise him up; when Chaitanya, during one of his fits, starts moaning and weeping, it is Gadadhar who tenderly wipes his face clean and holds him in his arms. While other disciples are noted for their learning or energy, Gadadhar is an unforgettable emblem of self-effacing love.

Although the conditions of travel between regions remain difficult and dangerous, especially because of sudden revivals of the conflict between the sultan of Bengal and King Prataparudra of Orissa, Chaitanya still receives visitors from distant parts, especially from his home town, Nabadwip.

The great chariot festival of Puri, Rathajatra, which takes place in the Bengali month of Asharh, is the time when the largest number of pilgrims and devotees make the journey to Puri. In the rare intervals when Chaitanya emerges from his transcendental reveries, he greets them with joy and love. He asks them to join him in sankirtan. Together, they walk around the streets of Puri, lifting their voices in a full-throated expression of their love for Krishna. Among these visitors, the ones who have known him longest – from his time in Nabadwip and during the initial period in Puri – feel blessed in being able to revive their connection with him. But do they also wonder at his physical deterioration, the emaciation of his once-robust form, the furrows made by tears and dust on his beautiful face? Does any one of them sense the irrevocable waning of an effulgent presence?

~

June 1533. Once again, it is the season of rain and rejuvenation in Bengal and Orissa. As usual, the town is humming with the presence of hundreds of pilgrims who have gathered to watch the annual nine-day festival of Rathajatra. Even the king, Prataparudra, is expected to be there. Three great wooden chariots, supported by enormous wheels carved from the wood of the local phasi tree, are constructed for the occasion. The images of Jagannath, Balabhadra and Subhadra will be placed in them and they will then make the traditional journey from the Jagannath temple to the Gundicha temple where they will stay for a week. Chaitanya has emerged from his meditative trance, and plans to lead his disciples as they walk along with the chariots. They will be singing kirtans, chanting the Hare Krishna mantra and dancing. This has been his practice in previous years and he is looking forward to it this year too, despite his increasing frailty.

His friends and followers have noticed lately that over and above his ecstatic trances, he has also been subject to frequent bouts of sorrowful tears, and they wonder what that portends. Perhaps, they try to reassure themselves, being part of the festival will lift him out of his melancholy. They assume he will spend the greater part of the week near the Gundicha temple as he has done in previous years. Smaller than the main Jagannath temple, this is one of Chaitanya's favourite places. Except in the week of the festival, it does not house a deity, but its premises are always sacrosanct and its uninhabited space has an unusual spiritual aura. As the time for the festival draws near, the priests start the formal cleansing and purifying of the space within and around the Gundicha temple. Chaitanya enthusiastically takes part in this activity, as he has done in previous years. With heartfelt devotion, he wipes the walls and sweeps the floors, sometimes using his own clothing to gather up the dust and debris that have accumulated there. From time to time, silent tears flow down his cheeks. He dries his face with his scarf and then uses that scarf to wipe the temple wall. He reminds observers of a lover who has been parted from his beloved for a long time and whose anticipation at the thought of reunion flows out in those copious tears. But nothing in Chaitanya's conduct is self-centred. Engaging in this humblest of tasks, he also hopes to be an example to others – Brahmins and non-Brahmins – who lead lives of ease, bolstered by the presumption that manual domestic labour is only for the lower classes. By working side by side with the temple servants, Chaitanya hopes to demonstrate his faith in the equality of all men in the eyes of Krishna.

The Gundicha temple houses the three deities for the festive week, but during an interim three-day period it also serves as the venue for a unique performance of raas lila, a celebration that includes recitals from Sanskrit texts and the divinely erotic verses of the *Gita Gobinda* describing the love play between Krishna and Radha and the gopis of Brindaban. Although raas lila is celebrated later in the year in Brindaban and Mathura, it is a joyful part of the Rathajatra festival in Puri to which Chaitanya and other Krishna devotees look forward in eager anticipation. In their minds, the Gundicha temple becomes Brindaban during these three days. When he goes there at other times of the year, Chaitanya is touched by the redolence of that love which is beyond the realm of ordinary human possessiveness, the love that he has sought all his life. This year is expected to be no different.

Yet, it is different. The Rathajatra festival takes place during the waxing phase of the moon, but this year a dark mystery envelops the lives of

Chaitanya and his followers. Although no one can find the right words to speak or write about it, one stark fact remains undeniable – Chaitanya has vanished. In centuries to come, there will be endless speculation as to what exactly happened. Some will say he merged with the image of Jagannath. Some will wonder if he fell into the ocean and drowned. Others will say his foot was pierced by a sharp stone as he danced on the street and this caused an infection from which he died. Those most inclined towards fables will even come up with an absurd conspiracy theory about angry priests of the Jagannath temple, jealous of the Bengali monk's growing influence on the residents of Puri, murdering Chaitanya and burying him in a secret spot – a theory that is absolutely unrealistic given the high regard in which Chaitanya was held by both the king and eminent scholars in Puri. The legends, having been born, will gather momentum as they stream down the years, fed by numerous accounts – imaginary and factual – composed by disciples and followers. Eventually, scholars will try to decipher those texts to determine what exactly happened. But they will not be able to achieve a consensus.

None of that, however, is of real consequence. In the here and now of 29 June 1533, as well as in the endless stretch of future centuries, what matters is that a uniquely beloved figure who rejected the coldness of rigid orthodoxy and espoused the warmth of the devotee's single-minded aspiration for god's love, who, despite being the son of a Brahmin, opened his arms and his heart to all without regard for class or caste, is no longer to be found. His arrival on a night of eclipse nearly forty-eight years earlier had illuminated the world with a new light of hope. His disappearance under the light of a waxing moon is an eclipse that nothing can undo.

~

Or maybe, that is not so . . .

His chosen disciples, heartbroken as they are at the loss of their beloved guru, dedicate their lives to enshrining his message in the hearts and minds of people. Some of them, like Nityananda, carry out their mission in Chaitanya's native Bengal. They travel from village to village, town to town, speaking about their departed leader at gatherings small and large, urging listeners to join in singing the Hare Krishna chant in Chaitanya's favourite tunes, to turn away from the excesses of materialism and try to love their fellow human beings. When they encounter other committed Vaishnavs, they ask them to join in the task of furthering the mission of spreading Chaitanya's teachings far and wide. Another group, consisting of Rupa, Sanatan, Raghunath Bhatta, Gopal Bhatta and Raghunath Das, focus on writing about the master's life, faith and teachings for the benefit of generations to come. In later years, they will be joined in this endeavour by a younger acolyte, Jiva, the nephew of Rupa and Sanatan. Eventually, the followers of Chaitanya will refer to the six of them as the goswamis – keepers and teachers of knowledge. Following Chaitanya's instructions, the six movc away from Bengal and Orissa and settle in Brindaban. Apart from spreading the message of their departed leader, they also take on the task of revitalizing the old Vaishnav temples in Brindaban, Mathura and surrounding areas, many of which have been reduced to abandoned ruins during the long years of Muslim rule. The six goswamis know that if they succeed Chaitanya's words and thoughts will find a secure and holy sanctuary in these old temples made new, and uplift and provide comfort to visitors from all parts of India. Ever since they became Chaitanya's disciples, they have discarded the trappings of wealth, power and comfort that marked their earlier lives. Now they lead austere, monastic lives, single-mindedly pursuing their mission. They preach to all comers about Chaitanya's philosophy of bhakti. They motivate wealthy devotees to rebuild temples and shrines where Krishna will be worshipped and Chaitanya revered. And they record the details of Chaitanya's life as well as his thoughts and ideas in detailed texts which will become the scholarly bedrock of Gaudiya Vaishnavism.

In the process of transmission, the message acquires new elements, as is only to be expected. The goswamis, being human, differ in some of their perspectives, despite their unified dedication to Chaitanya, and their writings reveal these differences. Chaitanya, in his modesty, had never accepted the idea of being a divine incarnation, although there were times when, being in one of his trances, he did not refuse the devotional offerings of followers who perceived him as a god. Nor had he declared himself formally to be a guru or spiritual guide for individual disciples. What emerges from the writings of the goswamis, however, is a strong emphasis on the need for a guru to achieve spiritual insight. In their minds, Chaitanya is undeniably a guru, whose guidance and tutelage led them to glimpse the path to illumination and salvation. Now that he has departed, the goswamis feel that future devotees will also need to find a guru whose instruction will be vital for them to understand and internalize Chaitanya's message. Some of them acknowledge that even in this matter Chaitanya had expressed his liberality, once saying, 'Why should a guru have to be a Brahmin or a scholar and not a person from the lowest caste? To be a guru, all you need is to know Krishna.' Others, like Gopal Bhatta, retain some of the tenets of orthodoxy and declare that only a Brahmin or upper-caste person can serve as a proper Vaishnav guru. Despite such differences, however, the goswamis' writings form a coherent body of work that will become the pillars of the faith their master wanted to bring to all. During their lifetime, they will serve as admirable examples of selfless dedication and intense love for Chaitanya. And the flourishing philosophical and spiritual discourse generated by their writings will long keep alive the desire for a deep understanding of Chaitanya.

~

However, Chaitanya's continuing presence across the span of centuries will not solely be related to the work of scholars and philosophers. An intimate, visceral bond has always existed between him and the people of his native Bengal, a bond that time cannot erase. And this connection will declare its undying presence in the sound of kirtan music and the chanting of the Hare Krishna mantra that will resonate in the homes of residents throughout Bengal. Songs about Krishna and Radha, derived from the medieval lyrics of Joydeb, Vidyapati and Chandidas, which Chaitanya so loved to hear and recite, will be performed by gifted and dedicated singers to mark the Vaishnav festivals of Jhulan, or Janmashtami, or raas lila. Often such sessions will be prefaced by hymns invoking Chaitanya, Nityananda and his followers. And even in the sphere of the quotidian, as ordinary people start going about their business, some of them will begin the day chanting, '*Bhajo Gourango, kaho Gourango, laho Gouranger naam re . . .*'

~

No eclipse can hide the light forever. Mischievous Nimai, golden Gouranga, teacher and seeker Chaitanya – all remain tenaciously integrated with Bengali life and memory.

# Postscript

In the 1960s, an unusual sight could be seen in the streets of several large American cities – groups of men and women, dressed in saffron dhotis and saris, dancing and chanting the Hare Krishna mantra. Most of the men had shaven heads. Some played drums or small cymbals to accompany the chanting and many of them wore a beatific smile. When they took a break, they would approach passers-by and ask them to join them and chant the Hare Krishna mantra. They were the members of a revivalist Gaudiya Vaishnav movement led by a Bengali from Calcutta, A.C. Bhaktivedanta Swami Prabhupada (born Abhay Charan De).

The descendant of a Vaishnav family, Prabhupada was inspired by his own guru, Bhaktisiddhanta Sarasvati, to spread the message of Chaitanya all over the world. In 1960 he founded the International Society for Krishna Consciousness (ISKCON) in New York. The timing was serendipitous. Many young people in the West were rebelling against the status quo and the choices made by their previous generations. For them the novelty of ideas presented by Eastern cultures was immensely attractive. The powerful simplicity of Chaitanya's words as publicized by ISKCON, the idea that the path to god was not only reachable through the chanting of his name but was also accessible to all, Hindus and non-Hindus alike, resonated strongly among a wide range of people. Even a pop group like the Beatles took an interest and George Harrison became a devout follower of what people started calling the Hare Krishna movement. His song 'My Sweet Lord' is a heartfelt expression of his deep commitment to the Vaishnav path of worship.

Prabhupada was successful beyond his dreams. ISKCON grew rapidly and received huge donations from prospective members worldwide. It established schools and institutions to propagate the faith, both in the United States and in major Indian cities. As advised by his guru, Prabhupada concentrated not only on lecturing and proselytizing, but he also devoted considerable resources to creating what became the biggest publisher of Vaishnav texts worldwide. He also wrote numerous books himself. From its origin in the United States, ISKCON also spread to the United Kingdom. More than a hundred temples have been built by the organization where devotees come to worship and, in some cases, even to take vows as monks. During the festival of Rathajatra, ISKCON celebrates by organizing chariot processions in several American cities.

In India, ISKCON decided to build its headquarters in Mayapur, a Bengali town beside the Ganga. Modern Nabadwip, unlike the one described as Chaitanya's birthplace, is now located on the western bank of the river. According to ISKCON, it is Mayapur, on the east, which is the true birthplace of Chaitanya. The organization has used its significant resources and its clout to acquire an enormous expanse of land on which it has built residences for monks and devotees, temples, schools, a dairy farm and other associated enterprises. Its communal kitchens serve vegetarian meals to large numbers of people every day. Along the smooth, paved roads criss-crossing the ISKCON campus, bicycles and motorized carts carry the organization's members as well as visitors to different buildings. On one side of the property, a huge temple, which, at a height of 340 feet, will supposedly be the largest Vedic temple in the world, is being built. Several times a day, prayers to Krishna are offered in the smaller temple and shrines.

The mission of keeping Chaitanya's words and thoughts alive is admirable and has met with exceptional success. But what would a sixteenth-century monk who gave up all comforts, who was so immersed in his quest for Krishna as to often be oblivious of his surroundings, make of this well-oiled machine? It is a question which, like that of Chaitanya's disappearance, still has to wait for an answer.

# Acknowledgements

I am indebted to several people who helped to make this book possible. First and foremost, Chiki Sarkar of Juggernaut Books led me to a project that I found unexpectedly gratifying. Partha Chatterjee, Professor of Anthropology and Middle Eastern, South Asian and African Studies at Columbia University, directed me to several books that documented the times and conditions in which Chaitanya lived and also examined the myth of Chaitanya in the light of reason. Richard Lesage, South Asia Librarian at Widener Library, Harvard University, went out of his way in helping me with inter-library loans.

As always, I am very grateful to my wonderful agent, Anne Edelstein, for the unique perspective she brought to bear on this project.

Gouri Chatterjee did what she has done many times – accompanying me on research trips, offering me different perspectives, patiently reading early drafts and always providing encouragement. Subhadra De took time out from her hectic schedule and numerous commitments to procure books from Calcutta which served as useful reference points.

Most of all, I feel privileged to have grown up with my grandmother, Prabhabati Mukerjee, who endured more than a fair share of the slings and arrows of fortune in the course of her long life. Through it all, she conducted herself by internalizing the humility, love and tolerance she saw personified in Chaitanya. Without trying, she showed me every day what it means to be a true Vaishnav.

# A Note on the Author

Chitrita Banerji, a food historian and novelist, grew up in Calcutta and received her master's degree in English from Harvard University. She is the author of several books on the food and culture of Bengal and India, including *Eating India*. She has written for publications such as *Granta*, *Gourmet*, *Gastronomica*, the *New York Times* and the *Boston Globe*, and received awards at the Oxford Symposium of Food and Cookery. Her novel, *Mirror City*, set in newly liberated Bangladesh, was published by Penguin in 2014. Chitrita Banerji lives in Cambridge, Massachusetts.

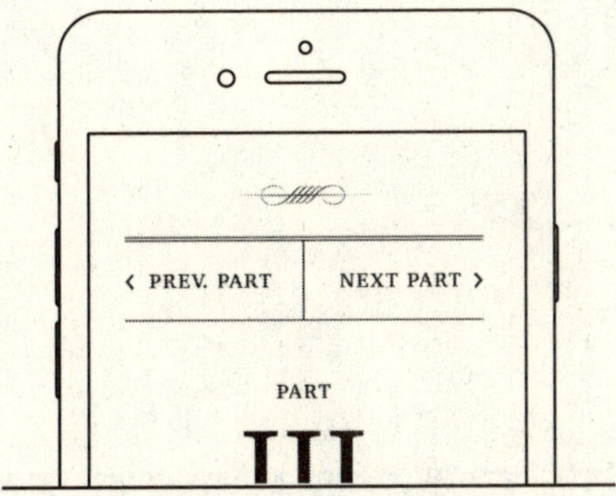


## Beautiful Typography

The quality of print transferred to your mobile. Forget ugly PDFs.

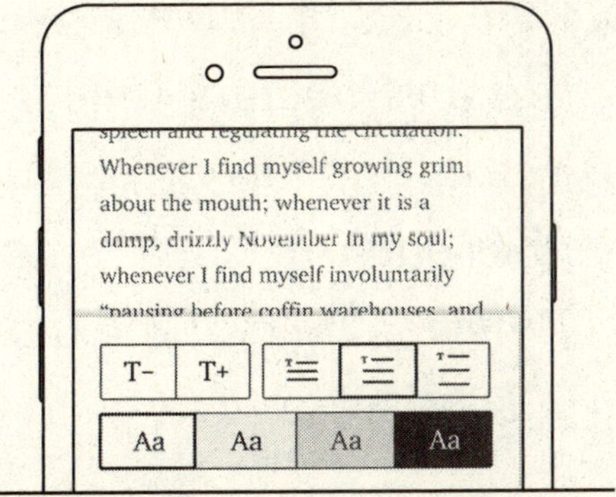


## Customizable Reading

Read in the font size, spacing and background of your liking.

# AN EXTENSIVE LIBRARY

*Including fresh, new, original Juggernaut books from the likes of Sunny Leone, Praveen Swami, Husain Haqqani, Umera Ahmed, Rujuta Diwekar and lots more. Plus, books from partner publishers and loads of free classics. Whichever genre you like, there's a book waiting for you.*

juggernaut.in

# DON'T JUST READ; INTERACT

*We're changing the reading experience from passive to active.*

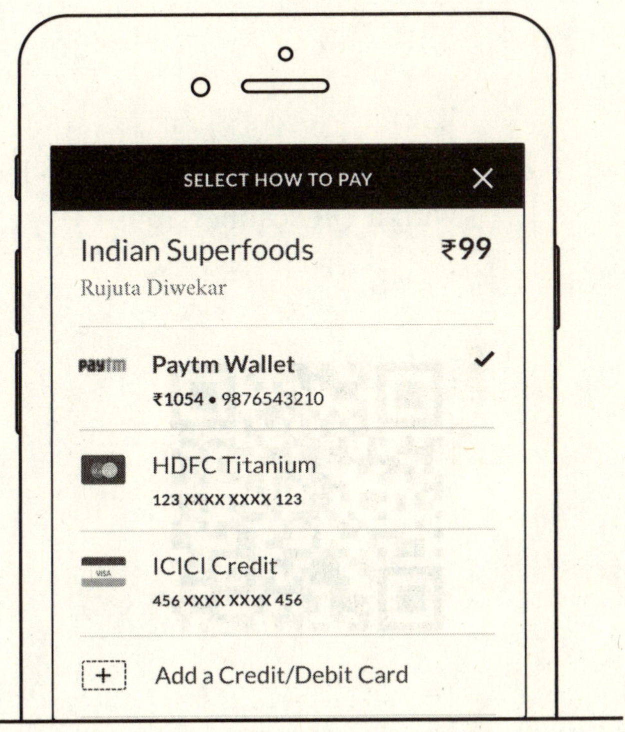


## Paytm Wallet, Cards & Apple Payments

On Android, just add a Paytm Wallet once and buy any book with one tap. On iOS, pay with one tap with your iTunes-linked debit/credit card.

To download the app scan the QR Code
with a QR scanner app